P · O · C · K · E · T · S

ROCKS &
MINERALS

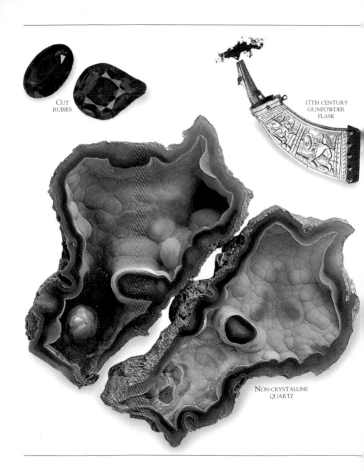

CUT
RUBIES

17TH CENTURY
GUNPOWDER
FLASK

NON-CRYSTALLINE
QUARTZ

P · O · C · K · E · T · S

ROCKS & MINERALS

Written by
SUE FULLER

GNEISS

WATCH
WITH BRASS
CASE

CHALCOPYRITE

DK

A DK PUBLISHING BOOK

www.dk.com

Project editor Neil Bridges
Art editor Diane Clouting
Senior editor Susan McKeever
Senior art editor Helen Senior
Designer Alexandra Brown
Picture research Caroline Brooke
Production Louise Barratt
US editor Jill Hamilton

First American Edition, 1995
8 1 0 9 7

Published in the United States by
DK Publishing, Inc.,
95 Madison Avenue, New York, New York 10016

Library of Congress Cataloging-in-Publication Data

Fuller, Sue
Rocks and minerals / written by Sue Fuller.
p. cm. — (A DK pocket)
Includes index.
ISBN 1-56458-663-4
1. Rocks—Juvenile literature. 2. Minerals—Juvenile literature. I. Title. II. Series.
QE432-2-F85 1995
552—dc20   93-48881
                                                                      CIP

Color reproduction by Colourscan, Singapore
Printed and bound in Italy by L.E.G.O.

CONTENTS

How to use this book 8

INTRODUCTION TO ROCKS AND MINERALS 10

Rocks and minerals 12
What are minerals? 18
What are rocks? 26

MINERALS 32

Colorless and white minerals
Diamond 34
Rock salts 36
Calcite 38
Barite 40
Gypsum 42
Beryl 44
Crystalline quartz 46
Noncrystalline quartz 48
Feldspars 50
Micas 52
Corundum 54

Silver and gray minerals
Silver 56
Platinum 58
Graphite 60
Galena 62

Yellow and gold minerals
Gold 64
Sulfur 66
Fool's gold 68

Green minerals
Malachite and azurite 70
Olivine 72
Tourmaline 74
Jade 76

Brown and red minerals
Copper 78
Hematite 80
Cassiterite 82
Mercury minerals 84
Sphalerite 86
Garnet 88

Purple and blue minerals
Fluorite 90
Turquoise 92
Lazurite 94

Black minerals
Magnetite 96
Amphiboles 98
Pyroxenes 100

ROCKS 102

Igneous rocks 104
Granite 106
Obsidian and rhyolite 108
Gabbro 110
Basalt and dolerite 112
Rocks from space 114

Metamorphic rocks 116
Gneiss and schist 118
Slate 120
Marble 122

Sedimentary rocks 124
Conglomerate and breccia 126
Sandstone 128
Limestone 130
Coal and oil 132

REFERENCE SECTION 134

Table of minerals 136
Mineral compositions 138
Mineral hardness 142
Geological timescale 144
Fieldwork safety and practice 146
Collecting rocks and minerals 148

Resources 150
Glossary 152
Index 156

HOW TO USE THIS BOOK

THESE PAGES SHOW YOU how to use *Pockets: Rocks and Minerals*. The book is divided into two main sections: minerals, followed by rocks. There is also an introductory section at the front, and a reference section at the back. Each section begins with a picture page, which gives an idea what it is about.

COLORS AND FORMATION
Minerals are arranged in the book by color. Rocks are arranged by the method in which they formed-igneous, metamorphic and sedimentary.

CORNER CODING
Corners of rock and mineral pages are color coded.

- COLORLESS AND WHITE MINERALS
- SILVER AND GRAY MINERALS
- YELLOW AND GOLD MINERALS
- GREEN MINERALS
- BROWN AND RED MINERALS
- PURPLE AND BLUE MINERALS
- BLACK MINERALS
- IGNEOUS ROCKS
- METAMORPHIC ROCKS
- SEDIMENTARY ROCKS

Corner coding

Heading

Introduction

Caption

MINERALS

GARNET

A GROUP OF silica-based minerals, garnets occur the world over, especially in metamorphic rocks. Geologists use garnets to identify rocks that have been altered by heat and pressure. A more everyday use is in jewellery. Purplish-red pyrope and red almandine garnets are most prized by jewellers.

Mass of twinned crystals

GROSSULAR GARNET
Pink and orange are common colours of grossular garnet, the lightest-coloured variety of garnet.

Similar colour to garnet

SIMILAR COLOUR
The name garnet may come from the Latin word for pomegranate, *granatum*. You can easily see the similarity of the colours of the glossy gemstones and the seeds of the fruit.

POMEGRANATE AND SEEDS

Symbol

HEADING
This describes the subject of the page. This page is about garnet. If a subject continues over several pages, the same heading applies.

INTRODUCTION
This provides a clear, general overview of the subject and gives you information that you need to know about it.

CAPTIONS AND ANNOTATIONS
Each illustration has a caption. Annotations, in *italics*, point out features of an illustration and usually have leader lines.

8

RUNNING HEADS

These remind you which section you are in. At the top of the left-hand page is the name of the section. The right-hand page has the mineral color, or rock type.

FACT BOXES

Most pages have fact boxes. These contain at-a-glance information about the subject. This fact box gives details such as the hardness, color, and luster of the mineral garnet.

SYMBOLS

These always appear next to the main mineral on the page. They refer to the crystal system that the mineral belongs to.

Running head *Fact box*

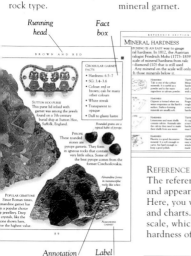

GROSSULAR GARNET FACTS

- Hardness: 6.5–7
- SG: 3.4–3.6
- Colour: red or brown; can be many other colours
- White streak
- Transparent to opaque
- Dull to glassy lustre

SUTTON HOO PURSE
This purse lid inlaid with garnet was among the jewels found on a 7th-century burial ship at Sutton Hoo, Suffolk, England.

Rounded grains are a typical habit of pyrope.

PYROPE
These rounded stones are pyrope garnets. They form in igneous rocks that contain very little silica. Some of the best pyrope comes from the former Czechoslovakia.

Almandine forms in metamorphic rocks like schist

POPULAR GEMSTONE
Since Roman times, almandine garnet has been a popular stone for jewellery. Deep crystals, like the stone shown here, have the highest value.

ALMANDINE GARNET

89

REFERENCE SECTION / MINERAL HARDNESS

MINERAL HARDNESS
ETCHING IS AN EASY way to gauge ... natural hardness from talc to diamond (10) that is still used ... Any mineral on the scale will only ... those minerals below it.

REFERENCE SECTION

The reference section pages are yellow and appear at the back of the book. Here, you will find useful facts, figures, and charts. These pages show Mohs' scale, which is a scale for measuring the hardness of minerals.

Annotation *Label*

LABELS

For extra clarity, some pictures have labels. They may give extra information, or identify a picture when it is not obvious from the text what it is.

INDEX AND GLOSSARY

You will find an index and glossary at the back of the book. The index lists virtually every subject and type of rock and mineral covered in the book. The glossary explains specialist words.

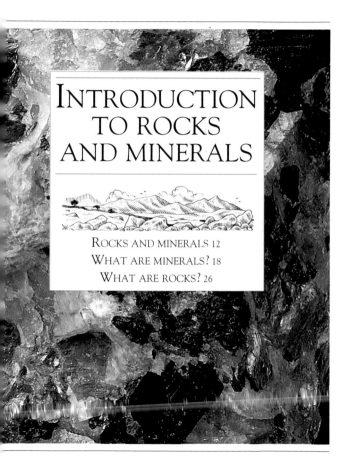

INTRODUCTION TO ROCKS AND MINERALS

ROCKS AND MINERALS 12
WHAT ARE MINERALS? 18
WHAT ARE ROCKS? 26

ROCKS AND MINERALS

MINERALS ARE SOLID mixtures of chemicals that each have a set of characteristics – just like a fingerprint. Groups of minerals bind together in various ways to form rocks. The Earth's crust (surface layer) consists of these rocks. Below, you can see a rock called granite and the minerals that make it up.

Mica

COARSE-GRAINED GRANITE

Quartz

QUARTZ
The most common mineral in the Earth's crust is quartz. It forms the gray matrix (mass of rock in which other crystals are set) in the granite specimen.

Feldspar

FELDSPAR
Another common mineral that often forms part of rocks is feldspar. The white crystals shown here are a variety of feldspar called microcline. In the granite specimen, the feldspar crystals have a pinkish color.

MICA

The third mineral that typically occurs in granites, including the specimen shown, is mica. It also forms part of many other rocks. Biotite, shown below, is a black, platelike mica that is soft enough to scratch with a fingernail.

A vein of white quartz and gold chalcopyrite cuts through this granite block.

MINERAL VEIN IN GRANITE

Rocks can contain veins of precious minerals. The gold areas in this granite block are chalcopyrite, an ore of copper. An ore is a material from which metals are extracted.

Tourmaline

CUT TOURMALINE

Precious gem minerals can also grow in rocks, especially in coarse-grained igneous rocks like granite. The large black crystals in the granite specimen and the cut gem shown here both consist of the mineral tourmaline.

PURPLE
TOURMALINE
GEMSTONE

GRANITE QUARRY

Rocks are quarried and mined for the minerals that make them up and the ores and gems they contain. They are also valuable themselves, for building and for aggregate (broken stone) for roads and railways. This granite quarry is near Slyudyanka, Russian Federation.

The Earth

Our planet is like an onion – it is made
up of a number of layers. At the Earth's
center is a metallic core. The next
layer is the mantle, consisting of
solid rock that flows slowly in
huge currents. We live on the
crust, the thin outer layer of
continents and oceans.

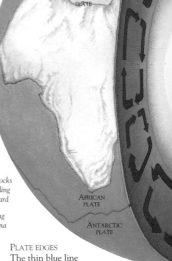

EURASIAN
PLATE

AFRICAN
PLATE

AFRICAN
PLATE

ANTARCTIC
PLATE

MOVING PLATES
The Earth's crust and upper mantle,
together called the lithosphere, are
broken up into nine pieces called
plates. At the edges of the plates,
new oceanic crust forms and is
destroyed. This causes the plates to
"float" around in the lithosphere. The
continents, such as Africa, form part
of the plates and they move with them.

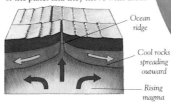

Ocean
ridge

Cool rocks
spreading
outward

Rising
magma

SPREADING OCEAN FLOOR
Oceanic crust forms at ocean ridges
where magma (molten rock beneath the
Earth's surface) rises and forms rock. As
more magma follows, rocks are pushed
sideways and the ocean floor spreads.

PLATE EDGES
The thin blue line
toward the bottom of the
diagram shows where the edges of the
African and Antarctic plates meet.

CORE

CRUST

MANTLE

COLLIDING CONTINENTS

When two continents collide, they crunch together to form mountain ranges. The European Alps and the Himalayas formed in this way.

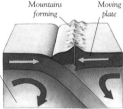

Mountains forming

Moving plate

Magma flow in mantle

AFRICAN AND EURASIAN PLATES

The blue line separating Africa and Europe on the diagram shows where the African and Eurasian plates have collided, bringing the two large continents together.

CRUST

The crust is a thin skin, only 43½ miles (70 km) deep at its thickest part. Beneath the oceans, the crust is much thinner, rarely more than 4⅓ miles (7 km) deep. The crust is cold and solid. It consists of continents and oceans.

CORE

A mixture of nickel and iron makes up the Earth's core. The inner core is solid and is about 2,510 miles (1,560 km) in size. The outer core is about 1,400 miles (2,220 km) deep. It is molten and moves. Movements in the outer core create the Earth's magnetic fields.

MANTLE

Solid rock circulates in huge, slowly moving currents inside the mantle. This layer is about 1,800 miles (2,900 km) thick and consists of minerals such as pyroxenes.

The age of rocks and minerals

Rocks and minerals have formed since the beginning of
time, and are still forming today. Written in these
solid materials is a full history of the
Earth. By studying rocks and minerals,
scientists have calculated the age of
the Earth and found out about
the great events that have
shaped our planet.

*Chondrite is made
up of small,
crystalline grains.*

OLDEST KNOWN ROCK
The oldest known rocks come
from outer space. This
chondrite specimen, for
example, is about
4.6 billion years old.
Although the Earth
formed at about the
same date, the first
rocks didn't develop
on our planet until later –
about 4.2 billion years ago.

ROCKS FORMING TODAY
New rocks are forming all the time, at the
Earth's surface and in the layers below.
This photograph taken from space shows
the Nile delta in Egypt. When the Nile
reaches the Mediterranean Sea, the
sediment carried by the river settles on the
seafloor. Over time, layers of sediment will
form new rock. This rock will provide a
permanent record of the environmental
conditions of the 20th century.

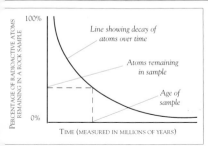

PERCENTAGE OF RADIOACTIVE ATOMS REMAINING IN A ROCK SAMPLE

100%

Line showing decay of atoms over time

Atoms remaining in sample

Age of sample

0%

TIME (MEASURED IN MILLIONS OF YEARS)

RADIOMETRIC DATING

Scientists have discovered a precise way of telling the age of rocks. It is called radiometric dating. Some radioactive atoms in rocks decay over time. By measuring the amount of these atoms remaining in a rock, scientists can calculate the age of the rock. This graph shows how to read this "geological clock."

This ammonite was preserved as a fossil in sedimentary rocks that formed during the early Jurassic period (see page 144).

FOSSIL RECORD

The first person to measure the age of rocks was the English engineer William Smith (1769–1839). He realized that fossils record the age of many types of sedimentary rock.

Inside, the ammonite shell was divided into chambers

WILLIAM SMITH

DATING FOSSILS

Everyone knows that the dinosaurs are extinct. They lived between about 245 and 65 million years ago. Any rocks that contain dinosaur fossils, therefore, must have formed between those dates. It is possible to date rocks quite accurately by studying the fossils they contain.

AMMONITE FOSSIL

WHAT ARE MINERALS?

ANIMAL, VEGETABLE, or mineral?
These three groups are often
used by people to describe
the world around them.
Minerals are solid,
regular mixtures of
chemicals. They have
characteristic
features that identify
them and can give
them value.

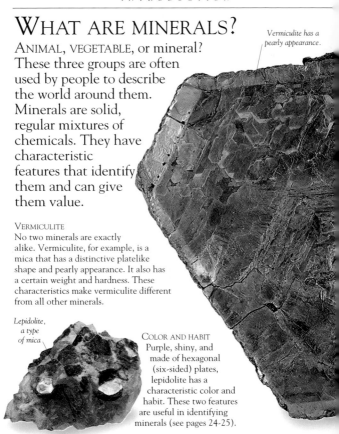

Vermiculite has a pearly appearance.

VERMICULITE
No two minerals are exactly
alike. Vermiculite, for example, is a
mica that has a distinctive platelike
shape and pearly appearance. It also has
a certain weight and hardness. These
characteristics make vermiculite different
from all other minerals.

Lepidolite, a type of mica

COLOR AND HABIT
Purple, shiny, and
made of hexagonal
(six-sided) plates,
lepidolite has a
characteristic color and
habit. These two features
are useful in identifying
minerals (see pages 24-25).

Distinctive platelike crystals

PATTERN OF ATOMS

The elements that make up a mineral build it in a rigid atomic pattern that is always the same. The atoms may form flat, loosely linked sheets or in tight spheres. Each pattern gives different properties to a mineral, such as color, shape, hardness, weight, and cleavage.

This model shows the atomic pattern of a mineral that is made up of thin sheets.

Thin sheets of mica

CLEAVAGE

Many minerals break along lines of weakness called cleavage planes. This mica breaks into thin sheets. It consists of strongly bonded silicon and oxygen atoms, separated by weakly bonded atoms of iron, potassium, and magnesium.

Sheets separated by cleavage planes

ROCK-FORMING MINERALS

Minerals grow or cement together to form rocks. This mica pegmatite (a rock with large crystals) consists of mica, quartz, and feldspar. These minerals formed rocks as magma cooled below the Earth's surface.

Large mica crystals

19

How minerals are formed

Minerals form in a huge range of environments – from human bones to the Earth's core. They grow from chemical ingredients called elements and may be affected by temperature and pressure as they develop. Some minerals, such as garnet, form over hundreds of thousands of years as heat and pressure gradually alter a rock. Olivine crystals, on the other hand, can grow several yards in an hour.

HEMATITE
(IRON ORE)

Bright red realgar crystals

REALGAR
(ARSENIC ORE)

GALENA
(LEAD ORE)

Metallic lustre

MINERAL VEINS
Hot water circulates in many places in the Earth's crust – beneath volcanoes and hot springs, for example. This water carries a rich load of dissolved minerals – just like a chemical soup. The "soup" deposits minerals as it cools, forming mineral veins in cracks or rocks cavities. These veins often contain valuable ores such as hematite, realgar, and galena.

METAMORPHIC MINERALS

New minerals grow when heat and pressure alter existing rocks, a process known as metamorphism. This happens, for example, in areas where mountains are forming. Metamorphic minerals often have a compact structure and a good crystal shape. They include precious gemstones such as garnet and spinel.

GARNETS IN SCHIST

SPINEL

IGNEOUS MINERALS

Magma and lava cool over time to form igneous rocks (see page 26). These rocks are made up of a small group of common minerals that share the chemicals of the magma. Magnetite and olivine are two minerals that form in igneous rocks.

OLIVINE

Olivine is transparent.

MAGNETITE

SEDIMENTARY MINERALS

Minerals can form at the Earth's surface. Evaporating sea water, for example, leaves behind minerals like sylvite. Calcite, which forms limestone rock, also develops in seawater and in the skeletons of many living creatures.

SYLVITE

CALCITE

White calcite crystals

Identifying minerals

Each mineral has a unique set of identifying properties. Six of the most important mineral properties are shown on the page opposite. To help you with identification, these six properties are featured in the fact boxes in the mineral section of this book. Minerals are also grouped into systems according their crystal symmetry (regularity of form). The yellow symbols shown below represent the main crystal systems.

CUBIC
Minerals grouped in the cubic crystal system have the most regular symmetry. The fool's gold mineral pyrite is a good example.

MONOCLINIC
Gypsum belongs to the monoclinic system. This is one of the most common systems, but has less symmetry than the cubic system.

TRICLINIC
Crystals in the triclinic system have the least regular symmetry of the crystal systems. Rare axinite belongs to this system.

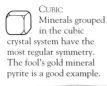

PYRITE

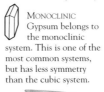

SELENITE
(VARIETY OF GYPSUM)

AXINITE

TRIGONAL/
HEXAGONAL
These two similar systems are commonly grouped together as one. The precious mineral beryl falls into this system.

ORTHORHOMBIC
Minerals in this system develop crystals that have a symmetry similar to that of a matchbox. Barite is a member of this system.

TETRAGONAL
Idocrase is a mineral in the tetragonal system. Crystals have a set of long sides and square ends, a little like a stretched cube.

EMERALD
(VARIETY OF BERYL)

BARITE

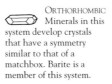

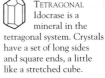

IDOCRASE

TALC

• SPECIFIC GRAVITY (SG)
You work out a mineral's
specific gravity by
comparing the weight of
the sample with the weight
of an equal volume of water.
Platinum has a specific
gravity of 21.4.

PLATINUM

• HARDNESS
The hardness of a mineral is
measured by how easily it
scratches. Mohs' scale is the
usual measure of mineral
hardness. Talc is the
softest mineral on the
scale. It has a hardness of 1.

CINNABAR
AND STREAK

• STREAK
If you crush a
mineral into a
powder, the color
of the powder is
known as streak.
Cinnabar has a reddish-
brown to scarlet streak.

AZURITE

BISMUTH

• COLOR
Azurite can
be identified by its
blue color. Other
minerals have many
colors and must be
identified in other ways.

CELESTINE

• TRANSPARENCY
A transparent
mineral, such as
celestine, allows light to
pass through it. Opaque
minerals do not allow any
light to pass through them.

• LUSTER
The way daylight reflects
off the surface of a
mineral is known as
luster. This bismuth
specimen has a shiny,
metallic luster.

2 3

Mineral color and habit

UNCUT RUBIES
AND SAPPHIRES

The beauty of minerals comes from their color and habit (shape). Some minerals have more than one color. For example, red ruby and blue sapphire are both varieties of corundum. By contrast, yellow is the only color of sulfur and is useful in identifying this mineral. Habit can also be a guide to identification. Malachite, for instance, typically forms bubbly masses and crusts. Corundum tends to develop well-formed crystals.

QUARTZ
Pure crystalline quartz is colorless. Colors appear when chemical impurities enter its crystal structure.

GYPSUM
Fibers of gypsum make up this specimen, which is pure in composition and colored white.

SILVER
Native silver often forms in a dendritic (branching) habit. Its characteristic color aids identification.

GOLD
Water-worn and rounded nuggets are one of the characteristic habits of valuable yellow gold.

SULFUR
This yellow mineral is idiochromatic – it gets its color because it only absorbs certain light rays.

TIGER'S EYE
This type of quartz has a silky appearance known as chatoyancy. Its colors resemble a tiger's eye.

RUBY
Tiny inclusions (other minerals enclosed in the crystal) give an attractive star effect in this red ruby.

TOURMALINE
This single crystal shows two of tourmaline's many colors, which are caused by chemical impurities.

MALACHITE
Only found in these green colors, malachite has a characteristic botryoidal (bubbly) habit.

TURQUOISE
This mineral always forms an encrusting or massive habit, which means it has no particular shape.

FLUORITE
Cubic crystal twins are a typical habit of fluorite. Twins are two crystals that are intergrown.

CLINOCLASE
Rare clinoclase grows in brilliant blue fibrous rosettes on the surface of other minerals.

HALITE
Errors in the atomic ⅃⅃⅃⅃⅃⅃ ⅃⅃ ⅃⅃⅃⅃⅃ ⅃ ⅃ specimen color it blue. Pure halite is white.

LABRADORITE
This ⅃⅃⅃⅃⅃⅃⅃ ⅃⅃⅃⅃⅃ ⅃ ⅃ ⅃⅃⅃⅃⅃⅃⅃ shows iridescence, a play of colors on its surface like a film of oil on water.

HEMATITE
⅃⅃⅃ ⅃⅃ ⅃⅃⅃⅃⅃⅃ is also iridescent and shows the unusual crystalline variety of the mineral.

WHAT ARE ROCKS?

CRUMBLY PEAT AND hard-wearing
granite may look and feel very
different, but they are both
rocks. Rocks are solid mixtures
of minerals. Geologists
classify rocks according to
the way they are formed.
The three main types are
igneous, metamorphic,
and sedimentary rocks.

Granite

GRANITE
(IGNEOUS ROCK)

IGNEOUS ROCK
Granite is an igneous rock. This rock type
develops as molten magma and lava cool. The
fragments of granite in the breccia formed
deep underground in the Earth's crust.

BRECCIA
This rock specimen is known as breccia. It is a sedimentary rock made from existing fragments of all three major rock types. Geologists can discover the history of this rock by studying these fragments.

OOLITIC LIMESTONE (SEDIMENTARY ROCK)

SEDIMENTARY ROCK
This rock is called oolitic limestone. It is a type of sedimentary rock that forms in seawater. Fragments of this type of limestone in the breccia indicate that the area in which the breccia formed was once covered by the sea. Sedimentary rocks record conditions at the Earth's surface.

Oolitic limestone

Folded gneiss

FOLDED GNEISS (METAMORPHIC ROCK)

METAMORPHIC ROCK
Gneiss is a metamorphic rock. It formed in conditions of great heat and pressure during mountain-building. Meta morphic rocks hold clues to processes that occur in the Earth's lithosphere.

2 7

The rock cycle

Heat, pressure, weathering, and erosion are some of the processes by which the Earth recycles rocks. The elements and minerals that make up rocks are never destroyed, but used many times over.

IGNEOUS ROCKS FORM

Liquid magma (1) cools and solidifies to form igneous rocks. This may happen deep underground in intrusions, such as dykes (2), or at the Earth's surface.

WEATHERING AND EROSION

Movements in the Earth's crust bring rocks to the surface. Agents such as wind, water, and ice break up the rocks into particles. This is weathering. Glaciers (3) and rivers (5) carry the particles from their original site. This removal process is called erosion.

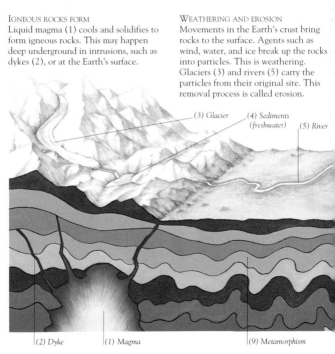

(3) Glacier (4) Sediments (freshwater) (5) River

(2) Dyke (1) Magma (9) Metamorphism

DEPOSITION AND METAMORPHISM

The rock particles may be deposited as sediments on land (6), in lakes (4), deltas (7), or farther out to sea (8). Strata, or layers of sediment, form as more material is deposited. The weight of successive layers of sediment compress and cement the particles. If the process stops there, sedimentary rocks are the result. Metamorphism (9) occurs if the rocks are deeply buried and heated. Heat and pressure transform old rocks and minerals into new.

ROCKS RECYCLED

Intense heat and pressure can melt rocks (11). This happens, for example, when two of the plates in the Earth's lithosphere collide (10). Molten rocks may form new magma. Some magma returns to the Earth's surface through volcanoes (12). It erupts as lava (13) and hardens to form new igneous rock. Magma may also be recycled in the crust. When this magma cools, it forms in igneous intrusions, such as dykes, and the rock cycle begins once again.

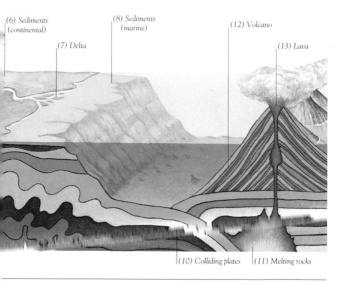

(6) Sediments (continental)

(7) Delta

(8) Sediments (marine)

(12) Volcano

(13) Lava

(10) Colliding plates

(11) Melting rocks

Identifying rocks

Rocks all have distinctive characteristics. You can often identify a rock specimen by making a few simple observations. All igneous and metamorphic rocks, for example, consist of interlocking crystals of different minerals. Crystals found in igneous rocks are usually randomly arranged. In metamorphic rocks, the crystals are often aligned into patterns, known as foliations. Sedimentary rocks are made of rock particles and minerals that are cemented together. On these pages, you can see some typical characteristics of igneous, metamorphic, and sedimentary rocks.

IGNEOUS ROCKS

GABBRO

BASALT

WHITE GRANITE

SLOW COOLING
Igneous rocks that form underground cool slowly. As a result, there is time for the rocks to develop large, well-formed crystals. Gabbro is an example of a slow-cooling igneous rock.

RAPID COOLING
Basalt is an example of an igneous rock that formed at the Earth's surface. It is similar to gabbro, but cools rapidly, and so consists of small, poorly developed crystals.

COLOR
Light-colored igneous rocks, such as this white granite, tend to be rich in silica. Dark-colored igneous rocks are usually silica-poor, but contain dark, heavy minerals.

METAMORPHIC ROCKS

SCHIST

SLATE WITH PYRITE

FOLDED GNEISS

FOLIATION
The action of pressure can align the crystals in metamorphic rocks. This gives rocks, such as this schist, a distinct foliated, or wavy, appearance.

PRESENCE OF MINERALS
Certain minerals grow in different conditions of heat and pressure. Pyrite often occurs in slate, for example. This rock forms in low heat and pressure.

SIZE OF CRYSTALS
Crystals grow slowly on metamorphic rocks. The large crystals in this gneiss indicate that it formed during long "cooking" in high heat and pressure.

SEDIMENTARY ROCKS

CONGLOMERATE

MILLET-SEED SANDSTONE

FRESHWATER LIMESTONE

PARTICLE SIZE
The size of particles in sedimentary rocks varies greatly – from the very coarse to the microscopic. Conglomerate is a rock that has coarse particles.

PARTICLE SHAPE
The shape of particles in sedimentary rocks shows how the particles have been transported. Desert winds rounded the particles in this sandstone.

PRESENCE OF FOSSILS
Fossils never occur in igneous rocks and only rarely in metamorphic rocks. They are common in many sedimentary rocks, such as this limestone.

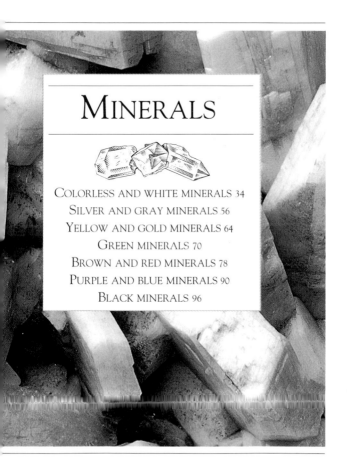

MINERALS

COLORLESS AND WHITE MINERALS 34
SILVER AND GRAY MINERALS 56
YELLOW AND GOLD MINERALS 64
GREEN MINERALS 70
BROWN AND RED MINERALS 78
PURPLE AND BLUE MINERALS 90
BLACK MINERALS 96

DIAMOND

THE FIERY brilliance of diamond makes it the most valuable gemstone in the world. People have worn diamonds as jewelry for centuries. It is also used in industry because it is the hardest naturally occurring mineral. Drills and saws that have diamonds in their tips can cut through any other substance.

COLORED DIAMONDS

NATIVE DIAMOND
Diamonds, like this one from South Africa, are found in a rare type of volcanic rock called kimberlite. They also occur in river gravels, where they can easily be mistaken for worthless pebbles.

CUBIC

Rough diamond

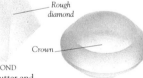

Crown

DIAMOND FACTS
- Hardness: 10
- SG: 3.52
- Color: colorless or white; can be many other colors
- White streak
- Transparent to opaque
- Adamantine (bright) to greasy luster

CUTTING A DIAMOND
A skilled stone cutter and polisher, called a lapidary, starts with a rough stone. Looking at the stone through a powerful lens reveals the grain (planes of cleavage) and finds any flaws and impurities that cutting must mask.

1 GRINDING DOWN
The lapidary removes the top pyramid of the rough diamond and rounds the stone by grinding it against another diamond. This is known as bruting.

Cut diamonds sparkle in this silver brooch.

DEEP FORMATION

Diamonds form in the Earth's mantle in conditions of extreme heat and pressure. At depths of about 93 miles (150 km), they develop a compact atomic structure that gives them their hardness. Volcanic eruptions bring the diamonds to the surface of the Earth.

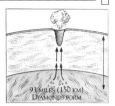

93 MILES (150 KM) DIAMONDS FORM

GRADING

Diamonds are graded by four properties: cut, clarity, color, and carat. These are known as "the four Cs." A carat is a measure of weight.

A brilliant cut

Facets cut in sets of four

4 BRILLIANT FINISH

A finished cut diamond with 57 facets is called a brilliant. (Model diamonds are used in this cutting sequence.)

Table facet

3 ADDING FACETS

Sloping cuts add facets to the diamond in sets of four, to both the top and bottom of the stone.

2 DOPS AND TABLES

Cutting continues with the diamond fixed tightly to a stick called a dop. The lapidary cuts a flat table facet (one side of a cut gem) using an iron grinding wheel coated with diamond dust.

CUTTING TOOL

The hardness of diamond makes it a powerful industrial cutting tool and abrasive. Oil well drilling bits and surgeons' scalpels have diamonds in their tips.

DIAMOND DRILL BIT

ROCK SALTS

HALITE AND SYLVITE belong to a range of minerals known as rock salts. These minerals form when salty water evaporates, and dissolve again if placed in fresh water.

Orange halite crystals

CUBIC

NATIVE HALITE
Halite is known commonly as edible salt, and is identified by its taste. It occurs around modern seas and lakes in hot, dry climates. Halite is also found below ground in areas where these conditions existed in the past. Beneath the North Sea, there are layers of halite that formed about 160 million years ago.

SALTY SEA
One of the world's most salty seas is the Dead Sea in the Middle East, seen here in a 19th-century engraving. It has so much salt dissolved in it that people can easily float on its surface. Rock salts form around the water's edge.

HALITE FACTS
- Hardness: 2
- SG: 2.1–2.2
- Color: white, orange, red, purple, blue, black
- White streak
- Transparent to translucent
- Glassy luster

POT OF
BLE SALT

DIAPIRS
Sheets of rock salt (1) that
formed millions of years
ago can flow upward under
pressure (2) toward the
Earth's surface. They form
domes called diapirs (3)
that can trap valuable
reserves of oil and gas
(shown by black areas).
Diapirs can be many
miles across.

ELEMENTS FOR LIVING
The elements sodium and
chlorine make up halite.
Both are essential for life, but
they are poisonous on their
own. Combined
in halite, they
are harmless.

SYLVITE
Bitter-tasting sylvite is less
common than halite. It
forms as the last dregs
of salt lakes and seas
evaporate. Sylvite
is a good source
of potassium,
an element
that is used
to make
fertilizers.

*Stepped
faces on
halite crystal*

*Sylvite occurs in
many colors, but
always has a
white streak.*

*Transparent,
cubic crystals*

HOPPER CRYSTALS
Cubic rock salt crystals can grow quickly from
saturated solutions. Sometimes, the crystals
grow faster along their edges than on their
faces. The result is a hopper crystal, with
regular or stepped depressions on each face.

CALCITE

A ROCK FORMING mineral, calcite is found in limestone and most seashells. It is very common at the Earth's surface. Calcite dissolves in water and grows anywhere that water can reach.

Calcite "nail"

NAILHEAD CALCITE
This nailhead calcite formed in a mineral vein and is joined with galena, the lead ore. The calcite crystals in the stem of the "nail" have slightly different shapes from those in the head.

Crystal face

TRIGONAL/ HEXAGONAL

Oyster shell

SHELLS
Shellfish make their shells from calcite, which they take in from sea water. Some shells are lined with lustrous nacre - from which an oyster makes its pearls.

DOGTOOTH
A common form of calcite crystal is dogtooth. Its unusual name comes from its sharp, pointed shape. A dogtooth's base is irregularly formed.

Growing rock
Stalactites hang from the ceilings of limestone caves. They grow when calcite precipitates (forms thin deposits) from dripping water. In the warmth and low pressures of the caves, the water evaporates and leaves a small deposit of calcite. Stalagmites grow where the water drops to the floor.

Growth rings

Stalactites grow a few millimeters a year.

Calcite terraces
The Pamukkale Falls, Turkey, formed as calcite precipitated from hot spring water. The mineral hardened to form a succession of terraces.

Galena

Calcite facts
- Hardness: 3
- SG: 2.71
- Color: white or colorless, gray, red, brown, green, black
- White streak
- Transparent to opaque
- Glassy, pearly, or dull luster

Seeing double
An image seen through calcite appears double. The name of this optical effect is double refraction.

Double refraction in transparent calcite

BARITE

IF YOU PICK UP a sample of barite, you will be surprised at how heavy it feels. This mineral weighs much more than its crystalline form suggests. In fact, it is heavier than some metallic minerals. Barite has many uses in industry and everyday life.

COCKSCOMB BARITE
Barite forms in many environments, from hot volcanic springs to mineral veins. Its habits also vary greatly. This example is cockscomb barite. It is made up of platelike crystals that combine to form rounded masses.

CRYSTALLINE BARITE

ORTHORHOMBIC

GROUND BARITE
Barite crystals are soft and are easily crushed. Ground barite acts as a filler in paints and paper. It also keeps oil well drill bits cool and lubricated during drilling.

Pearly luster on surfaces of tiny, platelike crystals

BARITE FACTS

- Hardness: 3–3.5
- SG: 4.5
- Color: colorless to white; can be many other colors
- White streak
- Transparent to translucent
- Glassy to pearly luster

DESERT ROSE

Any mineral collector would be happy to own this barite desert rose. It formed in a desert environment when water evaporated quickly in dry heat. Impurities in the water were left behind and formed crystals like petals.

The high specific gravity of barite is a key identification feature.

Crystals that radiate from the center form "petals"

GYPSUM

PLASTER OF PARIS, alabaster, fertilizers, and some types of explosive all contain gypsum. This mineral develops at the Earth's surface. It forms wherever water evaporates and in the mud around hot volcanic springs. Gypsum is an extremely common substance that is mined on a large scale in many parts of the world.

SELENITE CRYSTAL

Crystals radiate from a central point

RADIATING CRYSTALS
Gypsum can form as fibers or needles that radiate from a central point. Known as daisy gypsum, this habit looks like petals on a flower. Several bunches of these "flowers" may grow in one gypsum bed.

Translucent gypsum twin

Crystal mass

DAISY GYPSUM

TWINNED CRYSTALS
Gypsum crystals often grow in twins. These are crystals of the same mineral that grow together, but in slightly different directions. Common types of gypsum twins are "fishtails" or "swallowtails," so called because of their forked shape. These crystals are from Winnipeg, Canada.

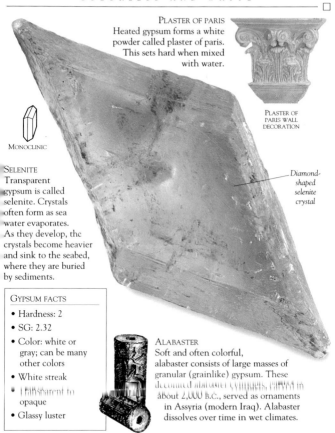

PLASTER OF PARIS
Heated gypsum forms a white powder called plaster of paris. This sets hard when mixed with water.

PLASTER OF PARIS WALL DECORATION

MONOCLINIC

SELENITE
Transparent gypsum is called selenite. Crystals often form as sea water evaporates. As they develop, the crystals become heavier and sink to the seabed, where they are buried by sediments.

Diamond-shaped selenite crystal

GYPSUM FACTS
- Hardness: 2
- SG: 2.32
- Color: white or gray; can be many other colors
- White streak
- Transparent to opaque
- Glassy luster

ALABASTER
Soft and often colorful, alabaster consists of large masses of granular (grainlike) gypsum. These decorated alabaster cylinders, carved in about 2,000 B.C., served as ornaments in Assyria (modern Iraq). Alabaster dissolves over time in wet climates.

BERYL

THE NAME AND VALUE of beryl vary, depending on its color. The pure mineral is colorless, but emerald and aquamarine are the best-known varieties. Beryl is rare and very hard, two qualities that combine with its fine colors to make it a desirable gemstone.

PRISMATIC CRYSTALS
Beryl forms deep in the Earth's crust. It most commonly occurs in granites and pegmatites (rocks with large crystals). These beryl crystals are prismatic, or longer in one direction than the other.

CUT BERYL GEMSTONES

COLORS
Small amounts of impurities give beryl its many colors. For instance, chromium or vanadium impart an emerald-green color. Manganese gives morganite (pink beryl) its color.

Morganite

TRIGONAL HEXAGON

HELIODOR
Iron gives heliodor its rich yellow color. This rare variety of beryl derives its name from the Greek word for the Sun, *helios*.

Emerald in ...ass of calcite crystals

Prismatic beryl crystal

EMERALD

Green beryl is known as emerald. The finest examples of this precious stone come from Colombia, where they have been mined for centuries. Other sources are Pakistan, Zambia, and Zimbabwe. This prismatic emerald lies in a bed of calcite crystals.

COLOR OF THE SEA

Aquamarine is the color of seawater, and that is the literal meaning of its name. Iron gives this variety of beryl its color. Aquamarine is less valuable than emerald, but was popular for jewelry in the 19th century.

Color given by small amounts of iron

BERYL FACTS

- Hardness: 7–8
- SG: 2.6–2.9
- Color: colorless or white when pure; can be many other colors
- White streak
- .... translucent
- Glassy luster

SPANISH EMERALDS

The Spanish introduced Colombian emeralds into Europe in the early 1500s. Many were treasures taken from the conquered .... and South America. This Spanish gold brooch dates from about 1650. It is set with 66 emeralds.

CRYSTALLINE QUARTZ

GOLDEN BEACH SAND and purple amethyst are both made of quartz. This mineral occurs in many rocks and is extremely common in the Earth's crust. Quartz crystals produce an electric charge if pressure is applied to them. This important property, known as piezoelectricity, gives quartz many uses and contributes to its value.

QUARTZ CRYSTALS

Crystals of quartz are common to most mineral collections. Typically, they have six sides and a top shaped like a pyramid. Quartz is a resistant mineral that represents hardness 7 on Mohs' scale. It is more hard-wearing than some gemstones.

TRIGONAL/
HEXAGONAL

CRYSTALLINE QUARTZ FACTS

- Hardness: 7
- SG: 2.65
- Color: colorless or white; can be many other colors
- White streak
- Transparent to translucent
- Glassy luster

MINERAL VEINS

Quartz often forms in mineral veins, such as these shown in a 19th-century engraving. Veins are cracks or faults in rocks into which hot, mineral-rich water flows. Quartz crystals develop as the water cools down.

Characteristic six-sided crystal with top shaped like a pyramid

AMETHYST
Purple quartz is called amethyst. Its color comes from tiny quantities of iron. Amethyst was very popular in 19th-century jewelry.

CITRINE
Slow heating turns amethyst into citrine, a yellow variety of quartz. Citrine rarely occurs in natural deposits and is a valuable collector's item.

DISCOVERY
The brothers Jacques and Pierre Curie discovered the property of piezoelectricity in quartz crystals.

RECORD PLAYER
Piezoelectric quartz crystals (hidden in a case in this picture) form part of a ~~~~~~~~~~~~~~~~~~ They turn vibrations caused by the stylus running through record grooves into an electric charge. Speakers then convert the electric charge into sound that people can hear.

Case holding quartz crystals

Stylus

NONCRYSTALLINE QUARTZ

CHALCEDONY IS THE NAME given to most
noncrystalline quartz. It describes agate,
jasper, carnelian, and chrysoprase. Other
varieties of noncrystalline quartz are flint
and opal. All these minerals develop
in cracks or cavities in rocks that
become filled with
quartz-rich water.

CHALCEDONY
Once split open, this rock from Brazil
revealed an inner secret. Its core is made
of chalcedony with a botryoidal
(grapelike) habit. A lining of brownish
agate surrounds the core.

BLACK
OPAL

TRIGONAL/
HEXAGONAL

SCATTERING LIGHT
Millions of tiny spheres
of noncrystalline quartz
make up opal. They reflect
and scatter light to give a
play of colors on the
surface of the mineral.

OPAL MINES
The fine colors in opal
make it a precious gemstone.
Most opal comes from
Australia, where it occurs in
sedimentary rocks. These
earth mounds are the result
of opal mining at Coober
Pedy, South Australia.

FLINT

One of the first materials used to make tools and weapons was flint. A tough substance, it chips easily and leaves sharp edges. This Beaker period (2,750–1,800 B.C.) dagger could have inflicted great harm.

CHALCEDONY FACTS

- Hardness: 7
- SG: 2.65
- Color: colorless or white; can be many other colors
- White streak
- Translucent or opaque
- Glassy or waxy luster

Botryoidal habit

Lining of brownish agate

BANDED CHALCEDONY

Agates are the banded variety of chalcedony. They usually grow in rings in rock cavities. The first ring forms on the wall of a cavity. Successive layers grow in parallel rings toward the center. Agates come in many colors. Brazil and Uruguay produce some of the best agates.

AGATES

Polished agate slice with colored bands

Agate grip

15TH-CENTURY PERSIAN DAGGER

FELDSPARS

A COMMON MINERAL group, feldspars form part of most types of rock, and occur in igneous, metamorphic, and sedimentary regions. Feldspar crystals vary greatly in size. Large examples can be up to 20 ft (6 m) long, while the smallest are microscopic. The uses of feldspars also vary – from fine jewelry to materials for building.

Mass of twinned albite crystals

Albite occurs in many types of rock

ALBITE FACTS

- Hardness: 6–6.5
- SG: 2.6–2.63
- Color: white; can be gray, green, pink, blue
- White streak
- Transparent to translucent
- Glassy to pearly luster

ALBITE
Granites, schists, and sandstones usually contain albite, an important variety of feldspar. Albite only rarely develops well-formed crystals like those shown here. A more usual habit is grains with no common shape.

TRICLINIC

Well-formed crystals
with flat tops

PIN SET
WITH
SUNSTONE

MOONSTONE
RING

FELDSPAR GEMS
Moonstone and
sunstone are gem-
quality feldspars.
Two types of feldspar
give moonstone its
white or blue
sheen. Some fine
examples come
from Myanmar, Sri
Lanka, and India.
The sparkle in
sunstone is caused
by light reflecting
off flakes of hematite.

Iridescence

IRIDESCENCE
Blocks of labradorite, a sodium-
rich variety of feldspar,
sometimes shows the optical
effect iridescence. This play
of colors is caused by
daylight reflecting off
layers of atoms deep
inside
this mineral.

BLUE
LABRADORITE

MICAS

PICK A TYPICAL metamorphic or igneous rock and it is likely to contain a mica. Micas are a common group of rock-forming minerals that can develop very large crystals. They are made up of sheets of silica that readily split like the pages of a book.

Flaky muscovite from Minas Gerais, Brazil

MUSCOVITE FACTS

- Hardness: 2.5–4
- SG: 2.77–2.88
- Color: white to grayish; can be many other colors
- Colorless streak
- Transparent to translucent
- Glassy to pearly luster

MUSCOVITE

White mica is known as muscovite, a mineral that forms part of many igneous and metamorphic rocks. Muscovite crystals can be impressive. The largest measure up to 13 ft (4 m) across, and single crystals can weigh 2 tons.

MONOCLINIC

PERFECT CLEAVAGE
Micas have perfect cleavage (break in only one direction), splitting into sheets along well-defined cleavage planes. This diagram shows the internal structure of a typical mica. You can see clearly the sheets that make up the mineral.

Thin sheets of mica

Micas break into sheets along cleavage planes.

SPLITTING ALONG PLANES
Abbé Hauy (1743–1822) was one of the first people to realize that crystals split into regular shapes along cleavage planes.

SPARK PLUG FROM 1935

Mica insulator

BIOTITE
A black mica, biotite contains large quantities of iron and magnesium. Radioactive elements are also present, which can be measured to give an estimate of the age of the biotite-bearing rock.

Broad, flat crystals

INDUSTRIAL USE
In the past, sheets of mica were widely employed in industry as insulators (materials that do not conduct electricity).

CORUNDUM

RUBIES AND SAPPHIRES are both rare and valuable forms of corundum. This mineral comes in many colors, but it is colorless when pure. Rating highly on Mohs' scale (9), corundum is very hard.

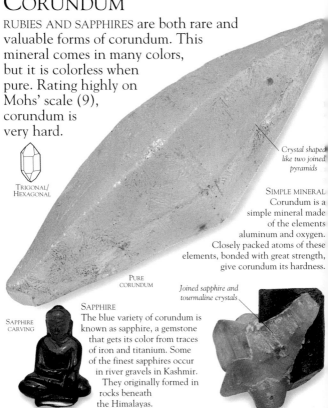

TRIGONAL/
HEXAGONAL

Crystal shaped like two joined pyramids

SIMPLE MINERAL
Corundum is a simple mineral made of the elements aluminum and oxygen. Closely packed atoms of these elements, bonded with great strength, give corundum its hardness.

PURE
CORUNDUM

Joined sapphire and tourmaline crystals

SAPPHIRE
CARVING

SAPPHIRE
The blue variety of corundum is known as sapphire, a gemstone that gets its color from traces of iron and titanium. Some of the finest sapphires occur in river gravels in Kashmir. They originally formed in rocks beneath the Himalayas.

HARD WORKER
The hardness of corundum makes it a useful mineral. Small grains are called emery, and are used in sandpaper. Many watches, such as this one, are set with rubies to protect their moving parts.

Flattened crystals are typical

Rubies set in wristwatch

RUBIES
True red corundum is called ruby. Traces of chromium gives this precious stone its color. The finest examples come from Myanmar, but Afghanistan and Pakistan are other sources. Rubies are most commonly found in river gravels.

CUT RUBIES

Ruby from the Mogok region of Myanmar

HEALING RUBIES
Some people believe that rubies can help to prevent illness.

PEACOCK THRONE
Thousands of precious gems adorned the famous Peacock Throne of Shah Jahan, a 17th-century ruler of Persia (today's Iran). Among them were 108 rubies.

CORUNDUM FACTS
- Hardness: 9
- SG: 4–4.1
- Color: colorless when pure; can be many other colors
- White streak
- Transparent to translucent
- Glassy luster

SILVER

BUNCHES OF WIRES and treelike branches are two
common habits of silver. This metallic mineral
can occur as a native element or mixed with
other minerals. The main source of silver today
is galena. Silver's value comes from its rarity
and many uses. Silver has been used for jewelry
and money since ancient times. Today, it
is also important in the photographic
and electronics
industries.

*Shiny, treelike
branches of silver*

NATIVE SILVER
When silver occurs in its
native form, it frequently
develops as bunches of wires.
Some of the finest examples of
this habit of silver come from the
area around Kongsberg, Norway.

BROWNIE
CAMERA

CUBIC

DENDRITES
Another common
habit of native silver
is treelike branches.
These are known as
dendrites. You can clearly
see the dendrites on this rock
matrix from the Northern
Territory, Australia.

PHOTOGRAPHY
The Brownie camera,
launched in the 1900s,
opened the photographic
era. Today, this pastime
an industry that consume
most of the world's silver

ORE CRUSHERS
Most of today's silver comes from ores such as galena. Crushing is the first stage in separating the mineral from its ore. These silver ore crushers are at Taxco, Mexico.

Metallic luster

Decorative scratches

SILVER BEAKER
This silver "portrait beaker" is from South America. Silver is soft enough to be beaten into shape and can be scratched to make decorative maps. These qualities have made silver a popular metal for jewelry and ornaments for centuries.

SILVER FACTS
- Hardness: 2.5–3
- SG: 10.5
- Color: silvery white
- Shiny, opaque... Opaque
- Metallic luster

PLATINUM

THE VALUE OF PLATINUM lies in its rarity and usefulness. This mineral is much rarer than gold and more valuable. Its uses include oil refining, reducing pollution from car exhausts, and jewelry. Platinum usually forms with nickel and copper deposits in igneous environments.

PLATINUM GRAINS

LARGE NUGGET
Platinum has a high specific gravity and does not alter during weathering. This means that it washes out of rocks and gathers in river gravels. A few large nuggets, like this example, have been found, but small grains are more common.

PLATINUM FACTS
- Hardness: 4–4.5
- SG: 21.4
- Color: silver to metallic gray
- Steel-gray streak
- Opaque
- Metallic luster

CUBIC

PLATINUM COINS
Like many precious
metals, platinum has
been used in coins.
The Russians struck
these platinum
coins during the
reign of Nicholas I
in the 19th century.

REDUCING POLLUTION
Catalytic converters reduce pollution
from cars. These devices contain tiny
amounts of platinum. The mineral
helps turn poisonous fumes from the
engine into less harmful
gases such as steam.

*Rugged
surface*

*Some of the finest
nuggets occur in
rivers running from
the Ural Mountains
in the Russian
Federation.*

*Metallic
luster*

GRAPHITE

DIAMOND AND GRAPHITE are both made of pure carbon, but have very different properties. Diamond is the hardest mineral, while graphite is one of the softest. Graphite can be cut with a knife and marks paper, hence its use in pencils. The difference between the two minerals is in their internal structures.

MASSIVE GRAPHITE
The usual habits of graphite are massive and thin skins on the surface of other minerals. Crystals rarely form. Graphite is a native mineral that occurs in metamorphic rocks, including altered limestone, schists, and coal seams.

FISSION
Huge graphite rods form part of the reactor core of some nuclear power stations, such as this one under construction. Power is generated by nuclear fission. This is when uranium atoms in the reactor split at high speed and release energy. The graphite rods help control the speed of fission.

Carbon atoms in bonded layers

GRAPHITE PENCIL

DIAMONDS

LAYERS OF ATOMS
This model of graphite shows strongly bonded layers of carbon atoms separated by weakly bonded layers. Graphite is soft because the strong layers slide over the weak.

Model of the internal structure of diamond, showing each atom bonded to four others

STRUCTURE OF DIAMOND
Like graphite, diamond is made up of carbon atoms. It is the way that these atoms fasten together, however, that gives diamond its hardness (10 on Mohs' scale). Each carbon atom in diamond bonds with four others to give a rigid structure.

Shiny surface

Graphite has a characteristic greasy feel

TRIGONAL/
HEXAGONAL

GRAPHITE FACTS
• Hardness: 1–2
• SG: 2.2
• Color: dark gray or black
• Gray black streak
• Opaque
• Shiny, wet luster

GALENA

SINCE ROMAN TIMES, galena has been a
valuable mineral, principally as the
ore for lead and silver. Galena is
a common mineral that
solidifies in hydrothermal
veins. These are cracks
in rocks at higher
levels in the Earth's
crust that fill with
hot, water-rich
solutions.

CUBIC
GALENA

CUBIC CRYSTALS
Galena usually
develops cubic
crystals and often forms
twins. "Steps" are another
common feature on broken
crystal faces. This specimen
clearly shows all
these properties.

CUBIC

*"Steps" on
broken crystal
faces*

SILVERY-GRAY COLOR
The broken face of
this sample of galena
reveals two features
of this mineral.
These are its
dark silvery gray
color and its cubic
crystal structure.

SPLIT
GALENA

BLOCK CLEAVAGE
Galena crystals cleave
into cubes or blocks along
three well-defined planes
of weakness, as shown in
this simple diagram.

Large mass of twinned galena crystals with shiny, metallic luster

Carved silver plaque showing a hunting scene

CAT'S WHISKER RADIO
Some radio receivers in the 1920s used crystals of galena. The radios, such as the one above, picked up a signal when the operator moved a thin copper wire against a galena crystal. The wire was often known as a cat's whisker.

SILVER ORE
Galena is a silver ore. There are about 2.2 lb (1 kg) of the valuable metal in 1 ton of galena. Silver has been used to make precious objects since ancient times. This silver plaque dates from about 1600.

Lead strips (cames) in a 19th-century window

FLEXIBLE METAL
Another useful mineral extracted from galena is lead. This metal melts and bends easily, making it ideal for seals and ᵽᵽᵽ lead was important in plumbing. Today, it is used for roofing and in windows.

GALENA FACTS

- Hardness: 2.5
- SG: 7.58
- Color: silvery gray
- ▪ ▪▪▪▪ ▪▪ ▪▪ ▪▪▪▪▪▪
- Opaque
- Metallic luster

GOLD

FEW MINERALS have the importance and value of gold. This rare native element has been used since ancient times as a measure and store of wealth. Gold is a dense, heavy metal with a high specific gravity, but it is soft and easy to work. Jewelers sometimes mix gold with other metals, such as silver and copper, to make it harder.

GOLD GRAINS

GOLD FACTS

- Hardness: 2.5–3
- SG: 19.3
- Color: bright yellow on fresh surfaces
- Golden-yellow streak
- Opaque
- Metallic luster

GOLD NUGGET
Few people will ever find a bright-colored gold nugget such as this example. Nuggets are extremely rare. They are usually crystalline and are often rounded at the edges due to weathering.

CUBIC

PANNING FOR GOLD
The prospect of finding gold started gold rushes in California and Australia in the 19th century. Prospectors pan river gravels for the metal in this engraving.

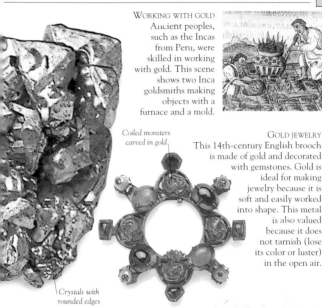

WORKING WITH GOLD
Ancient peoples, such as the Incas from Peru, were skilled in working with gold. This scene shows two Inca goldsmiths making objects with a furnace and a mold.

Coiled monsters carved in gold

GOLD JEWELRY
This 14th-century English brooch is made of gold and decorated with gemstones. Gold is ideal for making jewelry because it is soft and easily worked into shape. This metal is also valued because it does not tarnish (lose its color or luster) in the open air.

Crystals with rounded edges

GROWING ON QUARTZ
Gold and quartz often grow together in mineral veins when hot, watery liquids cool. The gold sometimes forms a crust on the surface of the quartz. Usually, it is spread throughout the quartz. Smelting (heating) separates the two minerals.

Gold crystals form a crust on quartz

SULFUR

POWDERED SULFUR

THE NATIVE ELEMENT SULFUR is a surprising mineral. It is poisonous, yet is used as a medicine. It is bright yellow, but burns with a blue flame if held over a lighted match. Sulfur is also a valuable mineral that is mined on a large scale. It forms around hot springs and volcanic craters. Deposits also occur near diapirs below the Earth's surface.

SULFUR CRYSTALS

Crystals are a common form of sulfur. They are soft and can be easily cut with a knife. Pure crystals are always yellow, but impurities can color them brown or black.

ORTHORHOMBIC

Crust of sulfur crystals on volcanic rock from Java, Indonesia

SULFUR MINING

Heated water is used to mine layers of sulfur around salt diapirs. It is pumped below ground into the mineral deposit. The sulfur melts in the water and is extracted at the surface by the use of compressed air.

STEAM VENT
Sulfur crystallizes around
volcanic vents and craters.
You can clearly see branches
of crystals at the opening of
this fumarole (steam vent).
They formed when hot,
sulfur-rich gases reached
the cool open air.

Sulfur-rich gas

VOLCANIC CRATER
A carpet of sulfur covers a
volcanic crater in Java.
Inside the crater, a
scientist wearing a mask
collects samples of gas rich
in sulfur. These samples
can hold clues to the
makeup of the rocks
inside the volcano.

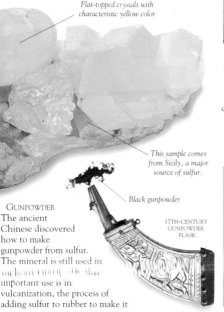

Flat-topped crystals with characteristic yellow color

This sample comes from Sicily, a major source of sulfur.

Black gunpowder

GUNPOWDER
The ancient
Chinese discovered
how to make
gunpowder from sulfur.
The mineral is still used in
my [...] [...] [...] [...] [...] important use is in
vulcanization, the process of
adding sulfur to rubber to make it

17TH-CENTURY
GUNPOWDER
FLASK

SULFUR FACTS

- Hardness: 1.5–2.5
- SG: 2–2.5
- Color: yellow;
  impurities may give
  it other colors
- White [...] [...]
- Transparent to
  translucent
- Greasy luster

FOOL'S GOLD

GOLD IS RARE and precious. There is, however, a common group of minerals that can be mistaken for gold. Known as fool's gold, these minerals are also valuable and beautiful in their own right. Pyrite, for instance, replaces bones and shells in fossils, and chalcopyrite is a valuable ore.

Crystal face with five sides

PYRITE CRYSTAL
There are several forms of pyrite crystal. Cubes are common, but this sample from the Italian island of Elba has 12 five-sided faces. The shape of the crystal depends on its growing conditions.

Ammonite cut in half to show its insides

PYRITE FOSSILS
Animals that lived many years ago often survive today as fossils. The ammonite shown here is preserved in pyrite.

Spear-shaped crystals in chalk

MARCASITE
Although the same elements that make up pyrite are found in marcasite, this mineral is less stable and decays in air. Newly found fossils made of marcasite crumble to dust if they are not properly cared for.

PYRITE FACTS
- Hardness: 6–6.5
- SG: 5
- Color: brassy to pale yellow
- Black streak
- Opaque
- Metallic luster

CHALCOPYRITE
An important metal ore, chalcopyrite has a more brassy color than pyrite and is much softer. This sample is made up of twinned crystals that have formed with white quartz.

Quartz crystals

COPPER ORE
This 19th-century diving helmet is made of copper, a metal that is extracted from chalcopyrite.

Lines, called striations, that form as crystals grow

Pale yellow color

CUBIC

CUBIC PYRITE

MALACHITE AND AZURITE

COPPER ROOFS TURN GREEN in the open air. The green material is malachite, which is an altered form of copper. When malachite replaces copper in ores underground, the mineral itself becomes a copper ore. It is then called a secondary ore. Azurite is also a secondary ore of copper. It has a characteristic bright blue color.

POLISHED MALACHITE
Bands of color make up this polished malachite slab. Malachite is a popular decorative materials that is used in buildings and ornaments. It takes a good polish, but dulls quickly because it is soft.

Specimen with typical dark green color and botryoidal habit

MONOCLINIC

ALTERED MINERAL
Copper minerals near the Earth's surface alter when exposed to water and cool temperatures. Malachite often forms in these conditions. Common habits are botryoidal lumps and tiny crystals. It always has a green color, which varies only in intensity.

Malachite is widely used as a decorative stone. It is also a secondary ore of copper.

MALACHITE FACTS

- Hardness: 3.5–4
- SG: 4
- Color: green
- Pale green streak
- Translucent to opaque
- Glassy or silky luster

Powdered malachite

Powdered azurite

GREEN AND BLUE
Malachite and azurite produce natural pigments. Bright green malachite pigment was known in ancient Egypt. Azurite grinds down to give a rich color called azure blue.

Azurite crystals

Tiny malachite crystals form a crust

AZURITE
Vivid blue azurite has almost the same chemical makeup as malachite, but contains less water. These two minerals often grow together, as they have done here.

Limonite

OLIVINE

THE NAME OLIVINE refers to a group of minerals that are found in igneous rocks. This group only forms in molten rock beneath the Earth's surface. Peridot is the best-known variety of olivine. It is a gemstone with an olive-green color and oily luster. The finest peridot specimens come from Zebirget in the Red Sea.

PERIDOT
CRYSTALS

PERIDOT
Gem-quality olivine is known as peridot. The ancient Greeks and Romans were among the first people to use this mineral for decoration.

OLIVINE FACTS
• Hardness: 6.5–7
• SG: 3.27–4.32
• Color: green or brown
• White streak
• Transparent to translucent
• Oily or glassy luster

FORSTERITE
Olivine contains varying amounts of iron and magnesium. The variety that only has magnesium present is called forsterite. This mineral can exist on its own, but it can also form a rock called dunite.

Mass of forsterite crystals

PELE'S
HAIR

WIRY ROCK
Golden brown "Pele's hair" is a
remarkable wiry rock made up of
tiny olivine crystals enclosed in
threads of basalt glass. It forms
during volcanic eruptions.

VOLCANIC BOMBS
An erupting volcano tosses volcanic bombs into
the night sky above the New Hebrides Islands
in the Pacific Ocean. The bombs are sticky
blobs of lava that harden into rock.
They can be broken open
to reveal green
olivine crystals.

Distinctive
oily luster

TRANSPARENT
PERIDOT

ORTHORHOMBIC

Peridot with a deep
green color is the most
valuable.

TOURMALINE

THE RANGE OF COLOR seen in tourmaline is the greatest of any mineral. Even a single crystal can have several colors. This mineral develops its complex chemistry in igneous and metamorphic regions. It also forms in mineral veins. Tourmaline can grow with other minerals such as beryl, quartz, and feldspar.

GREEN CRYSTAL
Different colors of tourmaline have different names. The green variety, shown here set in a mass of feldspar crystals, is called chromdravite. Pink rubellite and multicolored elbaite are other important varieties.

TRIGONAL/
HEXAGONAL

Mass of feldspar

LIKE A WATERMELON
This example is known as "watermelon" tourmaline because its colors are similar to those of the fruit. Impurities cause the colors in the crystal.

BLACK TOURMALINE

Schorl is the black variety of tourmaline. It is a common mineral in granite pegmatites and often occurs with quartz, feldspars, and micas. Iron-rich schorl crystals often have parallel grooves running down their sides. The specimen shown here is made up of schorl and white quartz crystals.

Schorl

Quartz

Poorly formed schorl crystals

JOHN RUSKIN

CHEMISTRY

The English philosopher John Ruskin (1819–1900) described the chemistry of tourmaline as being "more like a medieval doctor's prescription than the making of a respectable mineral!"

TOURMALINE FACTS

- Hardness: 7–7.5
- SG: 3–3.2
- Color: green; can be many other colors
- White streak
- Transparent to translucent
- Glassy luster

PLEOCHROISM

Tourmaline is a pleochroic mineral. This means that it looks a different color when viewed from different angles. These crystals, for example, appear green from the side. But they would appear black if you could turn them and look at them from above.

JADE

TOUGHER THAN STEEL, but soft enough to be carved, jade is rare and precious. It was first used for tools and weapons. Later, it was made into jewelry and ornaments. In 1863, the French scientist Damour showed that two different minerals shared the name jade. These minerals are called jadeite and nephrite.

JADEITE
A member of the pyroxene mineral group, jadeite forms in metamorphic rocks. The most valuable jadeite is known as "imperial jade."

Jadeite is an excellent carving material.

CARVED NEPHRITE
Both types of jade are excellent carving stones. They are tough materials that rarely crack or splinter because they consist of masses of tiny grains and fibers. This Maori "tiki," or good luck ornament, is made of nephrite.

MONOCLINIC

NEPHRITE SUIT

The family of a Chinese princess from the 2nd century B.C. laid her to rest in this ornate burial suit. It is made of nephrite plates linked by gold. The ancient Chinese believed that jade had the power to preserve life.

Large crystals rarely form in jadeite. This habit is massive.

NEPHRITE

More common than jadeite, nephrite is usually spinach-green. Other colors are gray and creamy white. Nephrite is a massive form of tremolite or actinolite, both members of the amphibole group. This sample is from New Zealand, a country where nephrite is mined.

Surface smoothed by erosion in water

Iron gives this example its green and brown color.

JADEITE FACTS

- Hardness: 6–7
- SG: 3.24
- Color: usually green; can be many other colors
- White streak
- translucent
- Glassy to greasy luster

COPPER

THE FIRST METAL to be separated from its ore and put to use was probably copper. People have worked this metal into weapons and tools for 8,000 years. It can be used on its own, or mixed with other metals like zinc and tin to form alloys. Copper rarely forms as a native mineral, and most commonly occurs in deposits of chalcopyrite.

COPPER ORNAMENT

NATIVE COPPER
A dendritic habit is typical of native copper. Fresh copper is a pale rose-red color, but it tarnishes quickly to copper-brown in contact with air.

Bundle of copper wires

NATIVE COPPER FACTS

- Hardness: 2.5–3
- SG: 8.9
- Color: copper-red or pale rose-red
- Copper-red streak
- Opaque
- Metallic luster

CYPRUS COPPER
The Mediterranean island of Cyprus, shown here, was the site of some of the earliest copper mines.

DEEP-SEA CABLE
An excellent carrier of electricity, copper is stretched into wires and used in deep-sea cables.

CUBIC

Branches of copper

COPPER ALLOYS
Familiar alloys of copper are bronze and brass. Bronze is a mix of copper and tin. It is a strong, durable metal that can be molded into different shapes. Brass is the combination of copper and zinc. This metal is usually a yellowish color.

12TH-CENTURY
BRONZE STATUE

GOOD FOOD
Tiny amounts of copper are present in many healthy foods, such as this whole-grain wheat.

CHALCOPYRITE

Massive habit

COPPER ORE
Chalcopyrite, a fool's gold mineral, is the main ore of copper. This practical metal has everyday uses in water pipes and electrical wiring.

PIECE OF
COPPER PIPE

HEMATITE

KIDNEY-SHAPED LUMPS and shiny black crystals are both common forms of hematite. This mineral is prized as an iron ore and as a gemstone. It develops in many rocks, from granites to limestones.

ROUNDED MASSES
The typical form of hematite is rounded masses, which look like animal kidneys. The name of this habit is reniform, from the Latin word for kidneys.

Metallic luster

TRIGONAL/
HEXAGONAL

REDDISH BROWN PIGMENT
Ground hematite makes a reddish brown pigment called ochre. It is one of the oldest natural pigments.

CHINESE MEDICINE
Some Chinese doctors treat their patients with powdered hematite mixed with red clay. They believe it is a useful medicine for certain illnesses.

HEMATITE FACTS

- Hardness: 5–6
- SG: 5.26
- Color: dull red or shiny black
  - Red streak
  - Opaque
  - Metallic to earthy luster

Iridescent hematite crystals

Stone lining hides steel framework

IRIDESCENCE
These hematite crystals from Elba show iridescence. It is caused by light bouncing off thin chemical films on the surface of the crystals.

Hexagonal (six-sided) crystals

Another name for reniform hematite is kidney ore.

SHINY SURFACE
This sample is called specular hematite, a semiprecious form of the mineral. The word specular describes crystals with shiny, reflective surfaces.

STRONG STEEL
Hematite is an ore of iron. This tough metal has many uses on its own, but is often converted to steel. Strong and flexible, steel is used in buildings such as the Empire State Building in New York.

CASSITERITE

MOST PEOPLE HAVE heard of tin. It is a common metal that has uses in industry and the home. The main ore of tin is cassiterite, a mineral that occurs in many parts of the world. Cassiterite forms in high-temperature hydrothermal veins and metamorphic rocks.

CRYSTALLINE CASSITERITE
Although cassiterite is a metal ore, it is unusual because it does not look metallic. Instead of being dull and opaque, crystals are shiny and translucent.

TETRAGONAL

GEMSTONES
Jewelers regard cassiterite as a semi-precious gemstone. Its qualities include hardness (between 6 and 7 on Mohs' scale) and the ability to hold a good polish. But even the finest cassiterite gems have flaws that affect their color – and hence their value.

SUPPLIES OF TIN
Disused buildings, such as this engine house, are all that remain of the tin mining industry in Cornwall, England. Up until the 19th century, the area was one of the most important sources of the metal. Its mines had operated for thousands of years. Today, Southeast Asia and West Africa supply most of the world's tin

Shiny luster is unusual for a metal ore

BRONZE HELMET
Tin readily mixes with other metals to form alloys. This Roman helmet from about 50 B.C. is made from bronze, the alloy of tin and copper. It is a strong metal that is resistant to rust. Pewter is the alloy of tin and lead.

LEGIONARY HELMET

Dark red color

Mass of twinned crystals

CASSITERITE FACTS

• Hardness: 6–7

• SG: 7

• Color: brown or black

• Dirty white streak

• Transparent to [illegible]

• Greasy to bright luster

HABITS
Crystals such as these are only one habit of cassiterite. Others are solid masses and nodules. In parts of Mexico, this mineral occurs as raspberry-shaped lumps known as wood tin.

Rock on which crystals have grown

MERCURY MINERALS

NATIVE MERCURY IS liquid at room temperature and is poisonous. Despite these curious properties, this metal has many commercial uses and is widely mined. Mercury can occur as a native element, but is most common in the mineral cinnabar.

Cinnabar is easily identified by its bright red color.

CINNABAR

Highly poisonous cinnabar is the main ore of mercury. This bright red mineral forms around volcanic vents and hot springs. It also occurs in mineral veins. Spain, Italy, and China have the largest cinnabar deposits.

TRIGONAL/
HEXAGONAL

Greasy luster

CINNABAR FACTS

• Hardness: 2–2.5

• SG: 8–8.2

• Color: red to brown

• Reddish brown to scarlet streak

• Transparent to opaque

• Greasy or earthy luster

VERMILION

Cinnabar is the main ingredient in the pigment vermilion. First used for painting in ancient China, its brilliant orange-red color was at the height of its popularity in medieval times. Today's paints are usually made from less poisonous substances.

THERMOMETER
Mercury's best-known use is in thermometers. These tools consist of a glass tube containing liquid mercury and a temperature scale. When the thermometer heats up, the mercury expands and rises up the tube. A reading can then be taken off the scale. This thermometer dates from the 18th century.

Bulb full of mercury

NATIVE MERCURY
At room temperature, mercury forms small blobs of silvery liquid. As a result, it is rarely found in its native state. Small deposits do occur, but are in high concentrations. Native mercury is opaque and has a bright metallic luster. Its high density is another identifying feature.

CLOSE-UP OF DEPOSIT OF NATIVE MERCURY IN ROCK CAVITY

SPHALERITE

SPHALERITE
GEMSTONE

THE MOST COMMON ORE of zinc is sphalerite. Also known as blende or "black jack," this mineral forms in hydrothermal veins with other ores such as galena. Some sphalerite is gem quality, but it is often too soft for a cut to last. The best stones have a deep reddish brown color.

UNCUT SPHALERITE
Sphalerite crystals such as this one are valued for their fine colors. After cutting, however, they wear down quickly and lose their sparkle.

MASSIVE
SPHALERITE

CUBIC

WORTHLESS MINERAL?
Early lead miners thought sphalerite to be worthless and threw it away. Now that its value is known, disused lead mines are reopening so that the sphalerite can be recovered.

Oysters are a good source of zinc.

Good crystals can be used to imitate diamonds.

SOURCES OF ZINC

Ores like sphalerite are not the only places where zinc is found. It also occurs in many foods. Good sources of zinc are eggs, whole-grain cereals, nuts, and seafood.

French bell-tower coated with zinc.

BUILDING MATERIAL

Galvanization is a major use of zinc. This is the process of coating iron and steel with zinc to protect them from rust. Zinc does not corrode (wear away or rust) easily, and is occasionally used as a building material.

Rough surface

Working parts made from steel, a tougher metal than brass

METAL ALLOY

Brass is an alloy of zinc and copper. An attractive metal that takes a good polish, brass is often used for decoration. The protective ring of this watch is made from brass.

SPHALERITE FACTS

- Hardness: 3.5–4
- SG: 3.9–4.1
- Color: brown or red; can be many other colors
- Will streak
- Transparent to translucent
- Greasy luster

GARNET

A GROUP OF silica-based minerals, garnets occur the world over, especially in metamorphic rocks. Geologists use garnets to identify rocks that have been altered by heat and pressure. A more common use is in jewelry. Purplish red pyrope and red almandine garnets are most prized by jewelers.

Mass of twinned crystals

GROSSULAR GARNET
Pink and orange are common colors of grossular garnet, the lightest-colored variety of garnet.

Similar color to garnet

POMEGRANATE AND SEEDS

CUBIC

SIMILAR COLOR
The name garnet may come from the Latin word for pomegranate, *granatum*. You can easily see the similarity of the colors of the glossy gemstones and the seeds of the fruit.

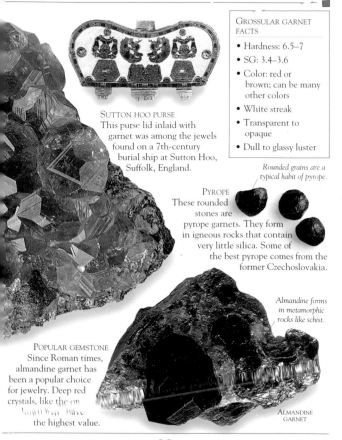

GROSSULAR GARNET
FACTS
• Hardness: 6.5–7
• SG: 3.4–3.6
• Color: red or
  brown; can be many
  other colors
• White streak
• Transparent to
  opaque
• Dull to glassy luster

SUTTON HOO PURSE
This purse lid inlaid with
garnet was among the jewels
found on a 7th-century
burial ship at Sutton Hoo,
Suffolk, England.

*Rounded grains are a
typical habit of pyrope.*

PYROPE
These rounded
stones are
pyrope garnets. They form
in igneous rocks that contain
very little silica. Some of
the best pyrope comes from the
former Czechoslovakia.

*Almandine forms
in metamorphic
rocks like schist.*

POPULAR GEMSTONE
Since Roman times,
almandine garnet has
been a popular choice
for jewelry. Deep red
crystals, like the on
the highest value.

ALMANDINE
GARNET

FLUORITE

THE COMMERCIAL VALUE of fluorite comes from its ability to melt easily. The origin of its name is also related to this property. It is derived from the Latin word *fluere*, which means "to flow." Fluorite is a common mineral that is found in hydrothermal veins and limestone

BLUE JOHN
Banded fluorite is known as Blue John. Its other name is Derbyshire Spar, after the English county in which it occurs. The bands vary in color from blue and purple to yellow.

COLORS OF FLUORITE
Purple cubes of fluorite are distinctive and widespread. This mineral also occurs in green, pink, and blue, but its only habits are crystalline or granular.

This green fluorite appears purple in ultraviolet light.

FLUORESCENCE
When invisible ultraviolet light shines on fluorite, the crystals appear to give off visible light in return. This is fluorescence. The fluorescent color of fluorite is often different from its daylight color.

FLUORITE FACTS
- Hardness: 4
- SG: 3.18
- Color: purple; can be many other colors
- White streak
- Transparent to translucent
- Glassy luster

FLUORITE IN STEELMAKING
An important industrial use of fluorite is in
steelmaking. It is added to the molten metal to
help it flow easily. At the same time, it removes
impurities like sulfur and phosphorus. This
worker is overseeing the steelmaking process at
a plant in Port Talbot, South Wales.

Glassy
luster

Transparency around
edges of crystal

PURPLE
FLUORITE

form as clusters of twins.
These twins are
octahedral, which means
they have eight faces.

CUBIC

TURQUOISE

FEW MINERALS HAVE been popular for as long as turquoise. First mined more than 6,000 years ago in the Sinai Desert in the Middle East, it is one of the best-known precious stones. Indeed, many people use the term "turquoise blue" to describe a certain shade of blue-green.

INSCRIBED TURQUOISE ORNAMENT

Crystals with dull luster

NATIVE TURQUOISE

Turquoise is a water-rich mineral that forms only in dry regions of the world. It develops in fine-grained masses, but never as large crystals. The finest turquoise comes from Iran, where it has been mined for 3,000 years.

CARVING TURQUOISE

Most of the world's turquoise deposits are in the southwestern United States. Over many centuries, people from the region have built up a reputation for carving attractive jewelry from local rock. This Indian worker from New Mexico carries on the tradition.

Turquoise forms a crust on this rock.

TURQUOISE INLAY
Many of the ancient peoples of
South America valued turquoise as a
precious carving stone. This gold
ceremonial knife handle is inlaid
with polished turquoise. It was
discovered in modern-day
Peru and dates from about the
13th century. The figure is
probably the image of a god.

COLOR
This selection
of polished stones
displays the instantly
familiar color of turquoise.
Copper, the common ingredient
of turquoise, gives the mineral
its color. Traces of iron tinge
the less valuable greenish variety.

TRICLINIC

TURQUOISE FACTS

- Hardness: 5–6
- SG: 2.6–2.8
- Color: bluish green
  with pale blue or green
  streak
- Opaque
- Dull or glassy luster

LAZURITE

THE MAIN INGREDIENT of ultramarine, the brilliant blue pigment, is lazurite. This mineral also dominates lapis lazuli, a rock prized for carvings and jewelry for thousands of years. Lazurite has a massive habit and is rare in nature. It is a metamorphic mineral that occurs only in marble.

NATIVE LAZURITE
A brilliant blue color characterizes native lazurite. The color comes from sulfur atoms, which are an essential part of its makeup. Lazurite is a silica-based mineral that develops in masses as heat alters limestone to marble.

White calcite crystals

LAPIS LAZULI VASE
Gold and precious stones decorate this spectacular lapis lazuli vase. It dates from the late 16th century. Lapis lazuli is hard enough to take a good polish and is very strong. The earliest lapis carvings are thousands of years old.

CUBIC

Sulfur gives lazurite its color

LAPIS LAZULI NECKLACE

Carved beads

LAZURITE FACTS
- Hardness: 5–5.5
- SG: 2.4–2.5
- Color: blue
- Blue streak
- Nearly opaque
- Dull or glassy luster

Paint made from ultramarine pigment

ULTRAMARINE
The ancient Persians were the first people to crush lapis lazuli and use it to make ultramarine.

Traces of brass-colored pyrite

Rough lapis lazuli with a high lazurite content

LAPIS LAZULI
Lapis lazuli consists of masses of lazurite mixed with calcite and pyrite. The higher the content of lazurite, the more precious the lapis.

Patches of blue lazurite

MAGNETITE

THE ANCIENT CHINESE MADE their first compasses from magnetite, an iron oxide that has natural magnetism. This mineral was also known to the ancient Greeks, who called it lodestone. Today, magnetite is important as an iron ore. It occurs in small quantities in many igneous rocks and meteorites. Some volcanic bombs also contain magnetite.

MAGNETITE CRYSTAL
Eight triangular faces make up this shiny magnetite crystal. Other habits of this mineral are massive and granular. Magnetite is a hard, heavy substance that does not fuse with other minerals. It does not cleave easily.

MAGNETIC COMPASS
Natural magnetism is one of the key identification features of magnetite. Magnetic materials attract small pieces of iron. They also deflect the needle of a compass. Seafarers have used magnetic compasses since the 12th century.

Compass point

MAGNETITE FACTS

• Hardness: 5.5–6.5
• SG: 5.2
• Color: black
• Black streak
• Opaque
• Metallic luster on fresh faces

LARGE DEPOSIT
Magnetite contains about 70 percent iron, making it a rich metal ore. One of the largest deposits of this mineral is at Kiruna, Sweden. Snow covers the huge opencast workings at Kiruna in this picture.

FORGED METAL
Iron is valuable once separated from its ore. The Romans forged iron into weapons and armor. Forging is the process of beating heated metal into shape.

ROMAN
LEGIONARY
ARMOR

Iron plates held together by leather straps

CUBIC

grains make up this sample of magnetite.

Dull, metallic luster

AMPHIBOLES

JUST LIKE DETECTIVES, geologists search for clues in the rocks they study. A typical "investigation" may begin with a group of minerals called amphiboles. These rock-forming minerals are useful to geologists because they record the conditions of temperature and pressure deep inside the Earth.

HORNBLENDE
Amphiboles grow in many igneous and metamorphic rocks, especially where water is abundant. Hornblende is a common member of this group. Its crystals are usually long and black with striations running down their sides.

MONOCLINIC

Coarse-grained amphibole crystals

AMPHIBOLITE
Hornblende often occurs in a rock called amphibolite. As its name suggests, this rock is made up almost entirely of amphiboles. It forms when metamorphism alters an igneous rock such as dolerite.

RHOMBIC CLEAVAGE
Amphiboles characteristically break into "slanted" blocks along planes of weakness. This is known as rhombic cleavage and is shown in this diagram.

WHITE AMPHIBOLE
Tremolite forms in marble and serpentinite (an igneous rock). Large deposits may be mined for a type of asbestos called mountain leather. This white tremolite sample has a plumose, or featherlike, habit.

GLAUCOPHANE
Sheaves of fibers and granular masses are the usual habits of glaucophane. This amphibole only forms in low temperatures and high pressures, usually as very hot rocks cool down. It often has a violet color.

Striations on side of twinned hornblende crystal

INTERLOCKING CRYSTALS
A common habit of riebeckite, shown here, is masses of long, interlocking crystals. They are usually dark blue to black in color. Riebeckite also occurs as bunches of fibers (known as crocidolite), which can be mined for asbestos.

HORNBLENDE FACTS

- Hardness: 5–6
- SG: 3.28–3.41
- Color: usually black; can be green and greenish brown
- White streak
- Translucent to opaque
- Silky to glassy luster

PYROXENES

THE MINERALS IN the pyroxene group form many of the Earth's rocks. They occur in igneous rocks, such as basalt, and make up most of the Earth's mantle. These minerals also form in metamorphic regions. You would even find pyroxenes in the rocks on the Moon if you could get there.

MONOCLI

AUGITE
The most common pyroxene is augite. It is a green to black mineral that forms in many basalts and gabbros. Augite rarely develops large crystals such as the one shown here, which comes from Italy.

Augite crystal

Rock mass made of smal crystals

PLATINUM MINE
This South African platinum mine is on the world's most valuable mineral lode (vein of metal ore). The lode cuts through pyroxenite, a rock entirely made up of pyroxenes.

AUGITE FACTS

- Hardness: 5.5–6
- SG: 3.23–3.52
- Color: black; can be various shades of brown and green
- Grayish green streak
- Transparent to translucent
- Dull to glassy luster

ENSTATITE

Meteorites and rocks in the Earth's mantle are rich in enstatite. This pyroxene often develops as fibers, but the specimen shown here has a crystalline habit. The crystals are translucent with a dark gray color.

DIOPSIDE

Dark green crystals with a glassy or pearly luster are a usual form of diopside. This mineral is the pyroxene most commonly found in metamorphic rocks. It also occurs in igneous rocks like basalt and gabbro.

Well-formed green crystals

AEGIRINE

Crystals and fibrous masses are the usual habits of aegirine. This is a wwwww mmm mmmmm mm mmm mmmmmm igneous and metamorphic rocks. Like all the other pyroxenes, aegirine has two cleavage planes that cross each other at right angles.

Striations on side of long crystal

ROCKS

IGNEOUS ROCKS 104
METAMORPHIC ROCKS 116
SEDIMENTARY ROCKS 124

IGNEOUS ROCKS

HOT, LIQUID MAGMA from the Earth's lithosphere
solidifies to form igneous rock. There are two main
types of igneous rock – intrusive and extrusive. The
intrusive type forms underground. Extrusive igneous
rocks solidify at the Earth's surface.

*Magma forces
its way through
existing rocks.*

PLUTON
Trapped magma
that cools deep
underground
forms a solid
igneous mass
called a pluton.
The size of
a pluton can
be impressive.
Some are hundreds
of miles wide.

Pluton

Magma chamber

SILICA CONTENT AND GRAIN SIZE
Igneous rocks are classified according to
the amount of silica in the minerals that
make them up. They are also grouped
by the size of their grains, or crystals. This table
shows a simple classification of igneous rocks
according to their silica content and grain size.

MAGMA CHAMBER
Large underground magma
chambers feed volcanoes at
the Earth's surface. When
these chambers cool, they
solidify to form plutons.

	HIGH SILICA	LOW SILICA
SMALL GRAINS	Obsidian	Basalt
MEDIUM GRAINS	Microgranite	Dolerite
LARGE GRAINS	Granite	Gabbro

GRANITE AND OBSIDIAN

Magma is the raw material of igneous rocks. It can come from the Earth's crust or directly from the mantle. Two rocks from the same magma source can look very different, however. Magma from an underground chamber cooled at the Earth's surface to form this block of obsidian. The granite specimen developed when the same chamber cooled to form a pluton.

Granite is an intrusive igneous rock. It has large crystals because it formed from magma that cooled slowly.

Obsidian is an extrusive igneous rock. It forms as lava cools very rapidly.

Layers of lava

Sill

SILL

Magma can slide between the bedding planes (layers) of sedimentary rocks. When this magma cools and hardens, it forms a feature called a sill. After erosion, sills appear at the Earth's surface as flat plates.

Volcano

Dyke

VOLCANO

Magma at the Earth's surface is called lava. It emerges through openings with a tube structure. The amount of magma affects the type of eruption. The higher the silica content of magma, the more violent the eruption.

DYKE

When magma cuts through existing rock structures, it may cool to form a dyke. This type of feature may form from the tube, or fissure, that links a magma chamber to a volcano.

GRANITE

IF YOU COULD DRILL deep into the Earth's crust on land, you would almost certainly find granite. This intrusive rock forms as magma cools slowly. Mineral veins filled with valuable metal ores often occur with granite, and coarse granites are a good source of gemstones.

WHITE GRANITE
Granite forms large grains as it cools. This rock typically consists of three silica-rich minerals – quartz, feldspar, and mica. Two types of feldspar, orthoclase and microcline, are dominant in this specimen and give it a light color. The dark grains are biotite mica.

Dark tourmaline crystal

GRANITE FACTS
- Origin: intrusive
- Occurrence: plutons
- Grain size: coarse to very coarse
- Color: light to medium
- Class: silica-rich

LARGE CRYSTALS
Pegmatites are rare granites that develop very large crystals. Gems often form in these rocks, as in this tourmaline pegmatite.

Large crystals formed as magma cooled slowly

GRANITE LANDFORMS

Tors are typical granite landforms that look like huge boulders stacked on top of each other. They became exposed as the surrounding rocks eroded away. This tor is on Dartmoor, in southwest England.

GRAPHIC GRANITE

Graphic granite contains strange gray quartz crystals. They have shapes like letters in an alphabet and form a series of lines. Graphic granite develops as magma cools under pressure.

Aligned quartz crystals

PINK GRANITE

Orthoclase feldspar dominates pink granite and gives this rock its color. Attractive granites such as this are comm... ...building stones, usually as polished decorative slabs. Crushed granite serves as a gravel and road-building material.

orthoclase feldspar

CARVING STONE

Granite is a hard-wearing ... ...statue of the Egyptian pharaoh Rameses II was carved from blocks of dark-colored granite.

OBSIDIAN AND RHYOLITE

VIOLENT EXPLOSIONS precede the formation of obsidian and rhyolite. These extrusive rocks form when magma with the same chemical makeup as granite reaches the Earth's surface. This magma is rich in silica, which makes it viscous (sticky). It traps gas that builds up and eventually causes a violent eruption.

OBSIDIAN

A simple way to describe obsidian is to call it "granite glass." Everyday glass, which is made from quartz sand, is a good comparison. Obsidian forms when lava cools so rapidly that crystals do not have time to grow.

Scattered snowflakes

SNOWFLAKE OBSIDIAN
White fibrous crystals can develop in obsidian, especially if the rock comes into contact with water. The crystals resemble snowflakes, giving this example its name.

OBSIDIAN FACTS

- Origin: extrusive
- Occurrence: volcanic
- Grain size: fine
- Color: black
- Class: silica-rich

Obsidian is usually black.

SCATTERED LAVA
The sulfur-rich springs at Rotorua, New Zealand, are the remains of a huge eruption. A gas cloud surged into the air, scattering lava all over the area. The lava hardened into rhyolite.

The bands in rhyolite often have different colors. The crystals that make it up are too small to be seen with the naked eye.

BANDED RHYOLITE
Rhyolite consists of swirls of crystals and glassy material. The crystals are fine-grained and contain quartz, feldspar, and mica. The bands in this specimen formed as lava flowed short distances after the eruption that brought it to the Earth's surface.

Smooth, glassy surface made up of minute crystals

OBSIDIAN SPEARHEAD
Fragments of obsidian have razor-sharp edges. They are also hard. These two properties made obsidian an ideal rock for early weapons such as this spearhead. It is from the Admiralty Islands, near Papua New Guinea.

Obsidian blade

GABBRO

A DEEP-LEVEL EXPLORATION of the Earth's crust beneath the oceans would reveal solid layers of gabbro. This coarse-grained rock forms when magma from the mantle cools. Rock collectors value gabbro specimens because the rock is relatively uncommon on land.

MINERAL MAKEUP

Gabbro is a silica-poor intrusive rock. It usually consists of feldspar, olivine, and members of the pyroxene group. Pyroxenes give this example its dark color. The light grains are a type of feldspar called plagioclase. Mineral veins are often found near gabbro masses in the Earth's crust.

Different minerals form light and dark layers.

GABBRO FACTS

- Origin: intrusive
- Occurrence: plutons
- Grain size: coarse
- Color: medium to dark
- Class: silica-poor

LAYERED GABBRO

Some gabbros form in layers made of single minerals. Magnetite makes up the dark layers in this specimen. The light parts are plagioclase feldspar.

Gabbro occurs in layers beneath the oceans.

ECLOGITE

A particularly silica-poor variety of gabbro is called eclogite. This rock is dominated by pyroxenes and garnet. These minerals form medium to coarse grains, and banding often occurs in the rock. Geologists think that eclogite resembles the chemical makeup of rocks in the Earth's mantle.

Banding in eclogite

Dark, coarse-grained pyroxenes

SERPENTINITE

Gabbros and eclogite break down in air and water over time. The remains of the minerals that made them up form a range of clays, which make up serpentinite. This rock varies in color from green to red. It is coarse-grained and often has bands. The large crystals in this example are green olivine.

GABBRO LANDSCAPE
The Black Cuillins of Skye, Scotland, consist of gabbro. These mountains have jagged ridges and steep sides. The rocks that make it up developed about 60 million years ago as the Atlantic Ocean formed.

BASALT AND DOLERITE

VIOLENT VOLCANIC eruptions are quite rare. Most eruptions are rather gentle events. Lava from the gentler volcanoes is runny and hardens into basalt and dolerite. These rocks are fine-grained equivalents of gabbro. They are also the most common rocks in the Earth's crust.

BASALT

Minerals that make up basalt include feldspars, pyroxenes, and olivine. They typically give this extrusive rock a dark gray to black color. The crystals in basalt are tiny.

Large crystal

PORPHYRITIC BASALT

Large crystals can form in basalt. They start to grow before they reach the Earth's surface in erupting lava. As the lava cools, a mass of smaller crystals traps the large crystals. They form a rock called porphyritic basalt.

BASALT FACTS

- Origin: extrusive
- Occurrence: volcanic
- Grain size: fine
- Color: dark
- Class: silica-poor

*You can see the
crystals in dolerite
with the naked eye.*

DOLERITE
A layer of dolerite lies beneath the
basalt on the ocean floor. Dolerite is
an intrusive rock that usually
forms in the Earth's crust. It has
coarser grains than basalt.

*Basalt is a
very common
extrusive rock.*

HAWAIIAN VOLCANO
The Kilauea volcano in Hawaii is a
basalt volcano. It erupts almost
continuously, but without
great explosions.

HOLES LEFT BY GAS BUBBLES
As lava hardens into basalt, gas
bubbles can leave rounded holes on
the surface of the rock. The holes are
called vesicles.

Basalt can form many-sided columns as
it cools. These columns are part of the
Giant's Causeway, in Northern Ireland.

*Rounded
vesicles in
basalt*

ROCKS FROM SPACE

OUR MOON, THE PLANETS, meteorites, and comets
all consist of rocks and minerals. Rocks from
space are clearly difficult to collect,
but the effort is worthwhile.
The reason is that
these rocks give us
clues about the way the
Earth formed about
4.6 billion years ago.

STONY IRON

Meteorites fall to Earth from space.
They are the remains of larger bodies
that have broken up in the Earth's
atmosphere. The example shown here
is a stony iron meteorite. It is made up
of silicate minerals, such as olivine,
and a nickel-iron alloy.

*Metallic
appearance*

MOON ROCK

Astronauts have returned to Earth with
many samples of Moon rock. These rocks
have been widely studied by geologists.
The most common type of rock on the
Moon is a variety of basalt that is also
found on Earth. This astronaut is collecting
rock samples on the Moon.

COMMON METEORITES

Chondrites are the most common meteorites. They are also very old, forming at about the same time as the Earth. Chondrites mostly contain minerals such as olivine and pyroxenes.

Mass of small, rounded grains

Pits created by heating during meteorite's fall

COMET

Some meteorites may be the remains of comets. These are huge "snowballs" made of ice, rock fragments, and gases that move around the Sun. Their tails can be millions of miles long. This picture shows the comet Kohoutek.

TEKTITES

When a meteorite hits the Earth, the intense heat melts fragments of the crust. Small blobs of molten rock fly out from the impact site, and harden to form rocks called tektites.

Smooth, shiny surface

BARRINGER CRATER

A giant meteorite about 656 ft (200 m) across created the Barringer crater, Arizona. The crater is 0.8 mile (1.3 km) wide.

METAMORPHIC ROCKS

EXISTING ROCKS ALTERED by heat and
pressure, or simply by heat alone,
are called metamorphic rocks.
The processes involved in
metamorphism are slow. As
the existing rocks are baked
and crushed, new minerals
gradually grow from the
chemicals present and
crystallize to form rock.

MAGMA
CHAMBER

THERMAL
METAMORPHISM

MAGMA CHAMBER
Metamorphism occurs
in many different
environments. For example, molten
rock in a magma chamber is much hotter
than the surrounding rocks. The heat from
the magma chamber bakes these rocks,
altering their form and mineral composition.

MARBLE

THERMAL METAMORPHISM
Rocks changed by the action of
heat alone are called thermal,
or contact, metamorphic
rocks. This process occurs
only where magma
breaks into existing rock
structures, such as in
plutons, dykes, and sills.
Marble is a thermal
metamorphic rock.

INCREASING DEPTH
The deeper a rock is
buried beneath the
Earth's surface, the
greater the heat and
pressure that act on it.
Heat increases because
the mantle bakes the
crust from below. Pressure
increases because of the
weight of the rocks above.

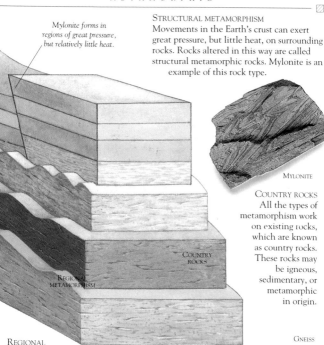

Mylonite forms in regions of great pressure, but relatively little heat.

STRUCTURAL METAMORPHISM
Movements in the Earth's crust can exert great pressure, but little heat, on surrounding rocks. Rocks altered in this way are called structural metamorphic rocks. Mylonite is an example of this rock type.

MYLONITE

COUNTRY ROCKS
All the types of metamorphism work on existing rocks, which are known as country rocks. These rocks may be igneous, sedimentary, or metamorphic in origin.

COUNTRY ROCKS

REGIONAL METAMORPHISM

GNEISS

REGIONAL METAMORPHISM
The most common type of metamorphism is when heat and pressure act together to alter a rock. This is called regional metamorphism. Deeply buried rocks and those in mountain building experience the greatest heat and pressure. Gneiss is a regional metamorphic rock.

GNEISS AND SCHIST

METALWORKERS MAKE USEFUL objects by heating metal and beating it into shape. In a similar way, heat and pressure deep beneath the Earth's highest mountains turn old rocks into new. Rocks known as gneisses and schists form in these conditions. Gneiss (pronounced "nice") is forged in higher heat and pressure than schist, but both rocks develop bands called foliations.

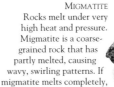

FOLDED GNEISS

Gneiss forms under high pressure and heat. These conditions change the minerals in existing rocks into new minerals. Gneisses are coarse-grained rocks with minerals arranged in bands. Quartz and feldspar make up the light bands in this folded gneiss. The dark bands are hornblende and biotite mica.

GNEISS FACTS

- Origin: mountain ranges
- Grain size: medium to coarse
- Pressure: high
- Heat: high
- Class: regional

MIGMATITE

Rocks melt under very high heat and pressure. Migmatite is a coarse-grained rock that has partly melted, causing wavy, swirling patterns. If migmatite melts completely, it becomes a granite.

GARNETS IN SCHIST

Minerals with a hard, compact structure develop in gneisses and schists. This group of red almandine garnets, for example, formed in a light-colored

Almandine garnet crystals

FOLDED SCHIST

Schists form in moderate heat and pressure. These rocks usually consist of medium-size crystals arranged in parallel layers. The foliations in this example developed as pressure acted on the rock from a single direction. Mica flakes give it a shiny surface.

Swirling in *a metamorphic rock partly melted in very high heat and pressure.*

Wavy bands of light and dark biotite mica

GREAT BEAR LAKE

Gneiss is the oldest known rock and forms low-lying landscapes that are dotted with lakes. A good example of this type of a gneiss landscape is the area around Great Bear Lake, Canada.

SLATE

TAP A BLOCK of slate with a hammer and chisel and it will split into thin plates. This property makes slate an important roofing material and chalkboard surface. Slate forms when the minerals that make up fine-grained rocks, such as clay and shale, are changed into mica. This change takes place at the edges of mountain-building regions where pressure and heat are relatively low.

GREEN SLATE
Microscopic crystals of mica give slate its shiny, wet appearance. Another mineral, chlorite, colors the green specimen shown here. The dark specks are grains of carbon and pyrite.

ROOFING MATERIAL
Mica crystals in slate are arranged in layers. The rock breaks into flat sheets along these layers. Sheets of slate serve as a roofing material, as on this house in Spring Lake, New Jersey.

BLACK SLATE

Carbon and pyrite give this slate specimen a dark color. The larger pyrite crystals form parallel lines like words on a page. You can also see how this example consists of layers that are separated by cleavage planes.

A layer of slate ends at this slightly raised edge. There is a cleavage plane between each layer.

SLATE QUARRY

Waste from a disused slate quarry near Blaenau Ffestiniog, North Wales, litters the hillside above this railway tunnel. Slate has been mined for centuries. Early miners used simple hammers and chisels to cut and split the rock.

SPOTTED SLATE

Most slate develops in mountain-building regions. Pre-existing slate may, however, be heated further by coming into contact with hot igneous rocks. This causes new minerals, such as cordierite and andalusite, to form in spotty patches.

Patches of randomly arranged cordierite

FOSSIL IN SLATE

Slate forms at such low temperature and pressure that fossils survive from the original rocks. This example comes from Devon, in England. It is known as a "Delabole butterfly."

SLATE FACTS

- Origin: mountain ranges
- Grain size: fine
- Na come too
- Heat: low
- Class: regional

MARBLE

THE ANCIENT GREEKS and Romans knew the value of marble. They used this perfect carving material to craft some of their finest statues and buildings. Marble forms when heat and pressure alter limestone. It is a common rock that occurs in mountain areas all over the world.

MARBLE CAPITAL

Coarse grains give a sugary appearance

WHITE MARBLE
Pure marble is white. It is the most prized carving and building stone. This unpolished specimen comes from near Malaga, Spain. Known as Mijas marble, it consists of coarse grains.

Colored streaks

GREEN MARBLE
Marble is altered limestone. Impurities from the limestone give marble its many colors, including red, pink, and green. Marble may have only one colour, or many colors in streaks or flowing patterns.

Greenish brown olivine mixed with calcite

OLIVINE MARBLE
A variety of minerals form in marble if the heated limestone contained flint. For example, this marble specimen is rich in olivine, which is more usually found in igneous rocks. The greenish brown grains of olivine are easy to see.

Marble consists of a mass of interlocking crystals. It is also a soft rock because it is largely made of calcite.

Decorative marble arcading

MARBLE TOWER
The Campanile, or Leaning Tower, in Pisa, Italy, has marble columns. Italy has some of the world's finest marbles.

MARBLE FACTS

- Origin: where heat and pressure act on limestone
- Grain size: variable
- Pressure: variable
- Heat: variable
- Class: thermal, regional

SEDIMENTARY ROCKS

BROKEN ROCK FRAGMENTS, seashells, and evaporites (minerals left behind by evaporation) are all materials that make up sedimentary rocks. These rocks form at the Earth's surface, in high mountains, deserts, and under the oceans. Geologists value sedimentary rocks because they provide an accurate record of the Earth's history.

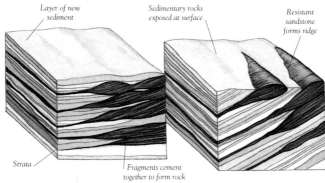

Layer of new sediment

Sedimentary rocks exposed at surface

Resistant sandstone forms ridge

Strata

Fragments cement together to form rock

LAYERS OF SEDIMENTS
Many sedimentary rocks are made up of fragments of other rocks. Agents such as wind, water, and ice deposit these fragments in layers called strata. More layers form, squashing the lower layers. Eventually, water-borne minerals cement the fragments together to form true rock.

ERODED ROCKS
Over time, buried rocks rise to the surface as the rocks above them erode away. Eroded rocks often form new rocks elsewhere. Some sedimentary rocks, such as sandstone, are more hard-wearing than others. When they reach the surface, they form distinct features, such as ridges.

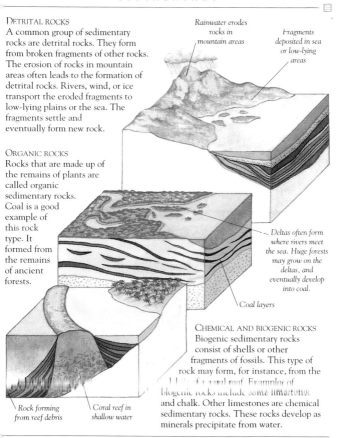

DETRITAL ROCKS
A common group of sedimentary rocks are detrital rocks. They form from broken fragments of other rocks. The erosion of rocks in mountain areas often leads to the formation of detrital rocks. Rivers, wind, or ice transport the eroded fragments to low-lying plains or the sea. The fragments settle and eventually form new rock.

Rainwater erodes rocks in mountain areas

Fragments deposited in sea or low-lying areas

ORGANIC ROCKS
Rocks that are made up of the remains of plants are called organic sedimentary rocks. Coal is a good example of this rock type. It formed from the remains of ancient forests.

Deltas often form where rivers meet the sea. Huge forests may grow on the deltas, and eventually develop into coal.

Coal layers

CHEMICAL AND BIOGENIC ROCKS
Biogenic sedimentary rocks consist of shells or other fragments of fossils. This type of rock may form, for instance, from the rubble of a coral reef. Examples of biogenic rocks include some limestone and chalk. Other limestones are chemical sedimentary rocks. These rocks develop as minerals precipitate from water.

Rock forming from reef debris

Coral reef in shallow water

CONGLOMERATE AND BRECCIA

PEBBLES AND LARGER blocks that become cemented together form conglomerate and breccia. The difference between these two rocks is the roundness of the pebbles, or clasts. Conglomerate has rounded clasts. By contrast, breccia has angular clasts.

FLINT CONGLOMERATE
Conglomerates may consist of many types of clast, or only one. This example, called puddingstone, has only flint clasts. Flint is a tough material that often occurs in sedimentary rocks.

Rounded flint clasts

Wooden handle

HARD ROCK
Conglomerate can be a very hard-wearing rock. Its hardness proved useful in this Roman corngrinder, which consists of two blocks of conglomerate and a wooden handle. The grain was crushed between the two blocks of rock.

CONGLOMERATE FACTS
- Origin: marine, freshwater, and continental
- Grain size: very coarse
- Grain shape: round
- Fossils: very rare
- Class: detrital

BRECCIA
Most breccias form in mountain areas, where the action of the Sun's heat and ice breaks rocks into coarse, sharp-edged clasts. This breccia contains clasts of different sizes, which are bound together by fine-grained sediments.

LIMESTONE BRECCIA
Clasts of igneous, metamorphic, and sedimentary origin occur in breccia. The large, angular fragments in this example are limestone. They are bound together by a light-colored "cement" that is rich in calcite.

Dark fragments of limestone

MELTING GLACIER
Mountains produce vast amounts of sediment as they erode. Much of this sediment gathers at the toes (ends) of glaciers, which are the most ꜰᷣ ⸱⸱⸱⸱⸱ ⸱⸱⸱⸱⸱⸱⸱⸱⸱⸱ ⸱⸱ ⸱⸱⸱⸱⸱⸱⸱⸱⸱⸱⸱ The debris at the toe of this glacier in Alaska may eventually form breccia.

SANDSTONE

MENTION THE WORD sand and many people will think of deserts and beaches. They may also think of sandstone, a sedimentary rock that is made of grains of sand. Sandstone forms in a range of environments and is often used as a building stone.

GRAINS IN SANDSTONE
Geologists define sandstone as a sedimentary rock that has grains between 0.02 and 2 mm in diameter. The grains are usually made of quartz, the most common mineral in sandstone.

Desert sand may one day form rock

Layers of fine grains

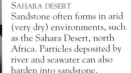

SAHARA DESERT
Sandstone often forms in arid (very dry) environments, such as the Sahara Desert, north Africa. Particles deposited by river and seawater can also harden into sandstone.

CARCASSONNE
Sandstone is a valuable building stone because it carves easily and resists weathering and pollution. The fortress city of Carcassonne, France, is largely built of this rock.

SANDSTONE FACTS

- Origin: marine, freshwater, and continental
- Grain size: medium
- Grain shape: angular, rounded
- Fossils: common
- Class: detrital

MILLET-SEED SANDSTONE
Grains of sand become rounded and polished in desert regions by the action of the wind. Eventually, the grains gather in layers that harden to form millet-seed sandstone. The dominant mineral in this example is quartz, but other minerals and rock fragments may be present.

Rounded grains characterize millet-seed sandstone

QUARTZ GRITSTONE
The sand grains in gritstone are more angular than those in millet-seed sandstone. Quartz makes up 75 percent of the rock, which comes from on land or in water. Gritstones often contain fossils, particularly if the rock consists of particles that were laid down in calm waters.

Angular-grained gritstone forms on land and in water.

LIMESTONE

THE REMAINS OF ANCIENT creatures make up many types of limestone. Other varieties form when minerals precipitate out of water. All limestones, however, form where water is present and consist mainly of calcite. The main uses of limestone include building stone, cement, and fertilizers.

Tiny, rounded ooliths

OOLITIC LIMESTONE

Like most limestones, oolitic limestone forms in seawater. Tiny, round balls called ooliths give this rock its name. Ooliths develop in warm, shallow seas when calcite precipitates on fragments of bone and shell. They grow as they roll back and forth in the waves.

LIMESTONE FACTS

- Origin: marine or freshwater
- Grain size: coarse to fine
- Grain shape: angular, rounded
- Fossils: common
- Class: chemical, biogenic

Coral colony preserved as limestone

CORAL LIMESTONE

The fossilized remains of coral make up this variety of limestone. Millions of years in the future, today's living corals, like the Great Barrier Reef, Australia, may develop into rock.

FRESHWATER LIMESTONE

Limestones are often rich in fossils, which give geologists precise information about the way in which the rock formed. This example contains the fossils of freshwater gastropods, or snails. They lived on the bed of an inland lake.

Shells bound together by fine-grained sediments

STONE FOREST

Limestone dissolves in rainwater, often creating spectacular landscapes. The stone forest of Kunming, China, is a fine example of eroded limestone.

Grains too small to see with a naked eye

CHALK

The skeletons of millions of tiny sea animals make up chalk, a form of marine limestone. The grains in chalk are usually too small to see without a magnifying glass.

BUILDING BLOCKS

Limestone is often used to make cement. This building, however, is built only from limestone blocks, with nothing binding them together.

COAL AND OIL

ROCKS ARE THE SOURCE of much of the world's energy. Coal is a sedimentary rock made from the plants that covered the Earth millions of years ago. Oil is the remains of microscopic marine plants and animals. It is often found deep below the ground in sedimentary rocks. Geologists use their knowledge of rocks to help track down reserves of these valuable energy resources.

COAL-POWERED STEAMSHIP

OIL SHALE
Shale is a rock made of clay that has been buried and compacted. Kerogen, a substance containing large amounts of carbon, often gathers in shale. When kerogen is heated, it gives off a vapor (gas containing moisture) that cools as oil.

Carbon gives coal its familiar dark color.

Oil shale, a fine-grained sedimentary rock

DRILLING FOR OIL
Most oil occurs as a liquid in underground rocks, known as reservoir rocks. The oil is held under pressure. When an oil rig, such as this one in the North Sea, drills into the reservoir rock, the oil flows to the surface.

Kerogen gathers in oil shale

Coal easily breaks into layers or blocks.

BITUMINOUS COAL

The plants of the ancient forest swamps are preserved in coal. Water preserved the vegetation, which gradually turned into bituminous, or household, coal. This hard, brittle rock is made up of about 60 percent carbon. When it burns, the other substances in coal form ash.

COAL-FORMING PROCESS

Plants are the raw materials of coal. Peat forms as layers of these dead plants become compacted. Compressed peat then becomes lignite, a low-quality brown coal. Further pressure turns lignite into bituminous coal, which is refined into high-quality anthracite under yet more pressure and heat.

LAYERS OF
WOODY PLANTS

COMPACTED
LAYER OF PEAT

LIGNITE
(30 PERCENT
CARBON CONTENT)

BITUMINOUS COAL
(60 PERCENT
CARBON CONTENT)

ANTHRACITE
(OVER 90 PERCENT
CARBON CONTENT)

COAL FACTS

- Origin: continental
- Grain size: medium to fine
- Grain shape: none
-
- Class: chemical, organic

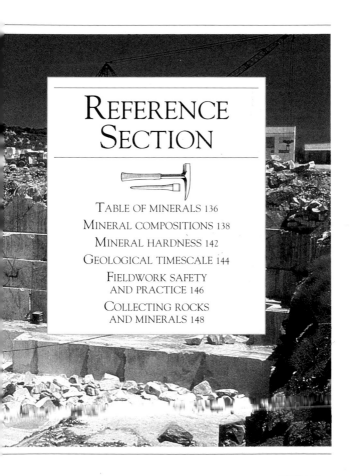

REFERENCE SECTION

TABLE OF MINERALS 136

MINERAL COMPOSITIONS 138

MINERAL HARDNESS 142

GEOLOGICAL TIMESCALE 144

FIELDWORK SAFETY
AND PRACTICE 146

COLLECTING ROCKS
AND MINERALS 148

TABLE OF MINERALS

THE MINERALS PRESENTED IN this book are listed below alphabetically. The first column gives a mineral's hardness on Mohs' scale. Its specific gravity (SG) is given in the second column. The last column highlights key features or properties of the mineral.

MINERAL	HARDNESS	SG	COMMENT/PROPERTY
Aegirine	6	3.55–3.6	Pyroxene; relatively rare group member
Albite	6–6.5	2.6–2.63	Feldspar; common in many rocks
Almandine	7–7.5	4.1–4.3	Gemstone; red garnet variety
Amethyst	7	2.65	Gemstone; purple variety of quartz
Aquamarine	7–8	2.6–2.9	Gemstone; bluish green variety of beryl
Augite	5.5–6	3.23–3.52	Pyroxene; common in many rocks
Azurite	3.5–4	3.77–3.78	Produces pigment known as azure blue
Barite	3–3.5	4.5	Crystals feel unusually heavy
Beryl	7–8	2.6–2.9	Gemstone; occurs in many colors
Biotite	2.5–3	2.7–3.4	Mica; usually has a dark color
Calcite	3	2.71	Rock former in limestone and marble
Cassiterite	6–7	7	Tin ore; has crystalline appearance
Chalcedony	7	2.65	Varieties include agate and jasper
Chalcopyrite	3.5–4	4.3–4.4	Fool's gold mineral; copper ore
Chromdravite	7–7.5	3–3.2	Gemstone; green variety of tourmaline
Cinnabar	2–2.5	8–8.2	Main ore of mercury
Citrine	7	2.65	Gemstone; yellow variety of quartz
Copper	2.5–3	8.9	Metallic element; conducts electricity
Corundum	9	4–4.1	Gemstone; extremely hard mineral
Diamond	10	3.52	Hardest naturally occurring mineral
Diopside	5.5–6.5	3.22–3.28	Pyroxene; common in many rocks
Emerald	7–8	2.6–2.9	Gemstone; green variety of beryl
Enstatite	5–6	3.2–3.4	Pyroxene; common in many rocks
Fluorite	4	3.18	Occurs in many colors; melts easily
Forsterite	6.5–7	3.27–4.32	Variety of olivine
Galena	2.5	7.58	Ore mineral of lead and silver

Mineral	Hardness	SG	Comment/property
Glaucophane	6	3.08–3.15	Amphibole; often has violet color
Gold	2.5–3	19.3	Precious metallic element
Graphite	1–2	2.2	Soft mineral made of pure carbon
Grossular	6.5–7	3.4–3.6	Gemstone; lightest-colored garnet
Gypsum	2	2.32	Used in plaster of Paris and alabaster
Halite	2	2.1–2.2	Commonly known as table salt
Heliodor	7–8	2.6–2.9	Gemstone; yellow variety of beryl
Hematite	5–6	5.26	Iron ore; produces ochre pigment
Hornblende	5–6	3.28–3.41	Amphibole; common in many rocks
Jadeite	6–7	3.24	Pyroxene; commonly known as jade
Labradorite	6–6.5	2.69–2.72	Feldspar; often shows iridescence
Lazurite	5–5.5	2.4–2.5	Main mineral in lapis lazuli
Magnetite	5.5–6.5	5.2	Iron ore; has natural magnetism
Malachite	3.5–4	4	Produces bright green pigment
Marcasite	6–6.5	4.92	Fool's gold mineral; decays in air
Mercury	Liquid	13.6–14.4	Metallic element; can occur as a liquid
Morganite	7–8	2.6–2.9	Gemstone; pink variety of beryl
Muscovite	2.5–4	2.77–2.88	Mica; common in many rocks
Nephrite	6.5	2.9–3.1	Amphibole; commonly known as jade
Olivine	6.5–7	3.27–4.32	Rock former; gem variety is peridot
Opal	5.5–6.5	1.9–2.3	Gemstone; valued for its rich colors
Platinum	4–4.5	21.4	Precious metallic element
Pyrite	6–6.5	5	Fool's gold mineral
Pyrope	7–7.5	3.5–3.8	Gemstone; purplish red garnet variety
Quartz	7	2.65	Most common mineral in Earth's crust
Riebeckite	5	3.32–3.38	Amphibole; common in many rocks
Ruby	9	4–4.1	Gemstone; red variety of corundum
Sapphire	9	4–4.1	Gemstone; blue variety of corundum
Schorl	7–7.5	3–3.2	Black variety of tourmaline
Silver	2.5–3	10.5	Precious metallic element
Sphalerite	3.5–4	3.9–4.1	Main ore of zinc
Sulfur	1.5–2.5	2–2.5	Burns with a blue flame
Sylvite	2	1.99	Potassium chloride
Topaz	8	3–3.2	Gemstone; occurs in many colors
Tremolite	5–6	2.9–3.2	Amphibole; can be mined for asbestos
Turquoise	5–6	2.6–2.8	Gemstone; excellent carving material

MINERAL COMPOSITIONS

THE COMPOSITION OF A mineral gives it properties, such as color and hardness. Some minerals consist of a single element. An example is diamond, which contains only carbon. Most minerals, however, are compounds or mixtures of elements. For example, quartz is a compound of silicon and oxygen.

Table of elements

The full table of elements is given below. The scientific symbols for the elements are in the left column. Their full names are given in the right column. The table lists the symbols in alphabetical order. Some of these elements appear in the list of mineral formulas on pages 140-1.

Symbol	Name	Symbol	Name	Symbol	Name
Ac	Actinium	Bi	Bismuth	Cr	Chromium
Ag	Silver	Bk	Berkelium	Cs	Cesium
Al	Aluminum	Br	Bromine	Cu	Copper
Am	Americium	C	Carbon	Dy	Dysprosium
Ar	Argon	Ca	Calcium	Er	Erbium
As	Arsenic	Cd	Cadmium	Es	Einsteinium
At	Astatine	Ce	Cerium	Eu	Europium
Au	Gold	Cf	Californium	F	Fluorine
B	Boron	Cl	Chlorine	Fe	Iron
Ba	Barium	Cm	Curium	Fm	Fermium
Be	Beryllium	Co	Cobalt	Fr	Francium

Symbol	Name
Ga	Gallium
Gd	Gadolinium
Ge	Germanium
H	Hydrogen
He	Helium
Hf	Hafnium
Hg	Mercury
Ho	Holmium
I	Iodine
In	Indium
Ir	Iridium
K	Potassium
Kr	Krypton
La	Lanthanum
Li	Lithium
Lr	Lawrencium
Lu	Lutetium
Md	Mendelevium
Mg	Magnesium
Mn	Manganese
Mo	Molybdenum
N	Nitrogen
Na	Sodium
Nb	Niobium
Nd	Neodymium
Ne	Neon

Symbol	Name
Ni	Nickel
No	Nobelium
Np	Neptunium
O	Oxygen
Os	Osmium
P	Phosphorus
Pa	Protactinium
Pb	Lead
Pd	Palladium
Pm	Promethium
Po	Polonium
Pr	Praseodymium
Pt	Platinum
Pu	Plutonium
Ra	Radium
Rb	Rubidium
Re	Rhenium
Rh	Rhodium
Rn	Radon
Ru	Ruthenium
S	Sulfur
Sb	Antimony
Sc	Scandium
Se	Selenium
Si	Silicon
Sm	Samarium

Symbol	Name
Sn	Tin
Sr	Strontium
Ta	Tantalum
Tb	Terbium
Tc	Technetium
Te	Tellurium
Th	Thorium
Ti	Titanium
Tl	Thallium
Tm	Thulium
U	Uranium
Une	Unnilennium
Unh	Unnilhexium
Uno	Unniloctium
Unp	Unnilpentium
Unq	Unnilquadium
Uns	Unnilseptium
V	Vanadium
W	Tungsten
Xe	Xenon
Y	Yttrium
Yb	Ytterbium
Zn	Zinc
Zr	Zirconium

Mineral formulas

The compositions of the minerals in the mineral section of this book appear below as formulas. A formula shows how different atoms make up a mineral. For example, halite (NaCl) is made up of sodium (Na) and chlorine (Cl) atoms.

Note: A subscripted number ($_2$) shows how many atoms of one element are joined to atoms of another element. For example, two oxygen atoms (O_2) are joined to one atom of silicon (Si) in quartz (SiO_2).

MINERAL	CHEMICAL FORMULA
Aegirine	$NaFeSi_2O_6$
Albite	$NaAlSi_3O_8$
Almandine	$Fe_3Al_2(SiO_4)_3$
Amethyst	SiO_2
Aquamarine	$Be_3Al_2Si_6O_{18}$
Augite	$CaNa(Mg,Fe,Al)(Al,Si)_2O_6$
Azurite	$Cu_3(CO_3)_2(OH)_2$
Barite	$BaSO_4$
Beryl	$Be_3Al_2Si_6O_{18}$
Biotite	$K(Mg,Fe)_3(Al,Fe)Si_3O_{10}(OH,F)_2$
Calcite	$CaCO_3$
Cassiterite	SnO_2
Chalcedony	SiO_2
Chalcopyrite	$CuFeS_2$
Chromdravite	$Na(Mg,Fe,Al,Mn,Li)_3Al_6(BO_3)_3(Si_6O_{18})(OH,F)_4$
Cinnabar	HgS
Copper	Cu
Corundum	Al_2O_3
Diamond	C
Diopside	$CaMgSi_2O_6$
Emerald	$Be_3Al_2Si_6O_{18}$
Enstatite	$MgSiO_3$
Fluorite	CaF_2
Forsterite	Mg_2SiO_4
Galena	PbS
Glaucophane	$Na_2(Mg,Fe)_3Al_2Si_8O_{22}(OH)_2$

MINERAL	CHEMICAL FORMULA
Gold	Au
Graphite	C
Grossular	$Ca_3Al_2(SiO_4)_3$
Gypsum	$CaSO_42H_2O$
Halite	NaCl
Heliodor	$Be_3Al_2Si_6O_{18}$
Hematite	Fe_2O_3
Hornblende	$NaCa_2(Mg,Fe,Al)_5(Si,Al)_8O_{22}(OH)_2$
Jadeite	$NaAlSi_2O_6$
Labradorite	$(Na,Ca)Al_{1-2}Si_{3-2}O_8$
Lazurite	$(Na,Ca)_8(Al,Si)_{12}O_{24}(S,SO)_4$
Magnetite	Fe_3O_4
Malachite	$Cu_2CO_3(OH)_2$
Marcasite	FeS_2
Mercury	Hg
Morganite	$Be_3Al_2Si_6O_{18}$
Muscovite	$KAl_3Si_3O_{10}(OH)_2$
Nephrite	$Ca_2(Mg,Fe)_5Si_8O_{22}(OH)_2$
Olivine	Mg_2SiO_4
Opal	SiO_2nH_2O
Platinum	Pt
Pyrite	FeS_2
Pyrope	$Mg_3Al_2(SiO_4)_3$
Quartz	SiO_2
Riebeckite	$Na_2Fe_3Fe_2Si_8O_{22}(OH)_2$
Ruby	Al_2O_3
Sapphire	Al_2O_3
Schorl	$Na(Mg,Fe,Al,Mn,Li)_3Al_6(BO_3)_3(Si_6O_{18})(OH,F)_4$
Silver	Ag
Sphalerite	ZnS
Sulfur	S
Sylvite	KCl
Tourmaline	$Na(Mg,Fe,Al,Mn,Li)_3Al_6(BO_3)_3(Si_6O_{18})(OH,F)_4$
Tremolite	$Ca_2Mg_5Si_8O_{22}(OH)_2$
Turquoise	$CuAl_6(PO_4)_4(OH)_8 \cdot 4H_2O$

MINERAL HARDNESS

SCRATCHING IS AN EASY way to gauge mineral hardness. In 1812, the Austrian mineralogist Friedrich Mohs (1773–1839) devised a scale of mineral hardness from talc (1) to diamond (10) that is still used today. Any mineral on the scale will scratch only those minerals with a lower hardness.

FRIEDRICH MOHS

1 TALC

HARDNESS
Talc is one of the softest minerals. It is useful as a powder and is the main ingredient in talcum powder.

TESTING
Minerals with a Mohs' hardness of 1 feel greasy and can be scratched with a fingernail.

2 GYPSUM

HARDNESS
Gypsum is formed when seawater evaporates at the Earth's surface. Surface-forming minerals are usually soft.

TESTING
Fingernails contain a tough protein that can scratch minerals with a hardness of 2.

3 CALCITE

HARDNESS
Limestones and most shells contain calcite. Animals take the calcite they need to make their shells from seawater.

TESTING
A copper coin will scratch minerals of hardness 3. The coin must be real copper.

4 FLUORITE

HARDNESS
Fluorite is a good decorative mineral. It is soft enough to carve, but hard enough to keep a good polish.

TESTING
Hardness 4 minerals are easy to scratch with window glass, which is made from quartz sand.

5 APATITE

HARDNESS
Human and animal bones are made from forms of apatite. It is a hard material that usually bends rather than breaks.

TESTING
Window glass will scratch minerals that have a hardness of between 5 and 6.

6 ORTHOCLASE

HARDNESS
Orthoclase is a type of feldspar. The gem variety of this mineral, moonstone, is one of the harder gemstones.

TESTING
A sharp piece of steel, such as a file, scratches minerals with a hardness of up to 6.5.

7 QUARTZ

HARDNESS
The most valuable gemstones are harder than quartz because they resist scratching by this common mineral.

TESTING
Quartz is too hard to scratch with everyday materials, but it can test softer substances.

8 TOPAZ

HARDNESS
Gem topaz is rare, but can form large crystals. Although it is hard, topaz breaks easily along a single cleavage plane.

TESTING
Minerals of hardness 8 and above are very rare, so scratch tests are not usually needed.

9 CORUNDUM

HARDNESS
This mineral has two valuable gem varieties, sapphire and ruby. Both are prized for their color and extreme hardness.

TESTING
Corundum leaves a mark on most other minerals on the scale, except diamond.

10 DIAMOND

HARDNESS
Diamond is the hardest mineral. It is many times harder than corundum, which is just below it on Mohs' scale.

TESTING
The only material that can scratch a diamond is another diamond.

GEOLOGICAL TIMESCALE

BY STUDYING ROCKS and fossils, geologists have built up
a history of the Earth. It is divided into periods, which
are shown in this spiral diagram. Our planet formed
about 4,600 million years ago (MYA) in the
Precambrian period. Many changes
have occurred since – changes
that are recorded in the rocks
and fossils of today.

CRETACEOUS (144–65 MYA)
The dinosaurs, including
three-horned *Triceratops*,
become extinct.

CAMBRIAN (550–510 MYA)
Boned animals develop, such
as this trilobite, *Xystridura*.

ORDOVICIAN
(510–438 MYA)
The first fishes
appear in shallow
seas.

DEVONIAN (408–362 MYA)
The seas fill with bony fish
like this *Pterichthyodes*.

SILURIAN (438–408 MYA)
Oxygen-forming plants
appear on land.

PRECAMBRIAN (4,600–550 MYA)
Simple plants and animals evolve.

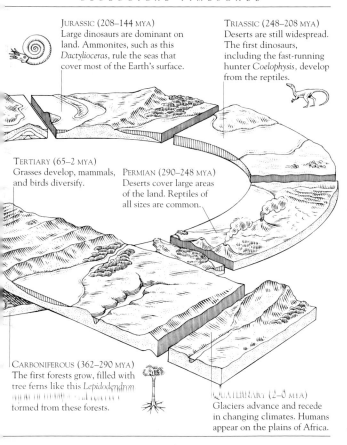

JURASSIC (208–144 MYA)
Large dinosaurs are dominant on land. Ammonites, such as this *Dactylioceras*, rule the seas that cover most of the Earth's surface.

TRIASSIC (248–208 MYA)
Deserts are still widespread. The first dinosaurs, including the fast-running hunter *Coelophysis*, develop from the reptiles.

TERTIARY (65–2 MYA)
Grasses develop, mammals, and birds diversify.

PERMIAN (290–248 MYA)
Deserts cover large areas of the land. Reptiles of all sizes are common.

CARBONIFEROUS (362–290 MYA)
The first forests grow, filled with tree ferns like this *Lepidodendron*. [illegible] formed from these forests.

QUATERNARY (2–0 MYA)
Glaciers advance and recede in changing climates. Humans appear on the plains of Africa.

FIELDWORK SAFETY AND PRACTICE

FIELDWORK IS PART of the enjoyment of collecting rocks and minerals. Your search for good specimens may take you to interesting places both in your locality and further afield. On a collecting trip, treat your chosen site with respect so that it can be enjoyed by others. You should also be aware of safety. These pages contain some simple tips for new collectors. It is also a good idea to seek the advice of experienced collectors or the national societies.

FIELDWORK CODE

• Do not go collecting alone. Join a local group with adult members.

• Make sure you take proper safety equipment on a collecting trip.

• Before setting out on a field trip, find out as much as possible about the intended collecting site.

• Always seek permission in advance for fieldwork on private, state or federally owned land.

• Be careful not to disturb or harm wildlife around the collecting site.

• Think about other collectors and leave sites tidy and safe.

• Collect specimens in moderation

• Do not leave behind or drop broken rock fragments – they may harm people and wildlife.

• Coastal sites, disused and working quarries, and cliff faces may be very dangerous for fieldwork. Avoid collecting from these sites unless you are under expert supervision.

• Always tell other people where you intend to go on a field trip, especially when collecting in potentially dangerous and remote areas like hills or mountains.

SAFETY ON SITE

Experienced rock and mineral collectors are very aware of safety. These are the typical things they take with them on every field trip:

• Protective clothing – warm, waterproof clothes and good hiking boots are essential.

• Safety equipment, including a hard hat, shatterproof goggles, and protective gloves. These must be worn at all times during fieldwork, particularly during hammering.

• A first-aid kit.

• Something to eat and drink.

SAFETY EQUIPMENT

STRONG
GLOVES

HARD
HAT

FIRST-AID KIT   PROTECTIVE GOGGLES

EQUIPMENT FOR RECORDING SAMPLES IN THE FIELD

SKETCHPAD
AND PENCIL

CAMERA

PHOTOGRAPHIC
FILM

OTHER POINTS TO REMEMBER

• It is often better to observe and record samples with a camera or sketchpad than remove them from a site. This leaves a site undamaged by hammering and preserves the sample.

• Only collect specimens when absolutely necessary and remove as few specimens as possible.

• Never collect from buildings, bridges, or walls.

• Don't tamper with machinery.

PENKNIFE

COINS

HAND LENS

IDENTIFYING A SPECIMEN

This simple kit may help you identify specimens found on site. After a close look with a hand lens, the penknife and coins will test the specimen's hardness.

COLLECTING ROCKS AND MINERALS

PLAN A COLLECTING trip in advance. It is a good idea to research the site and the sort of specimens you expect to find there. Good sites have abundant samples that can be collected safely and without harming the landscape. They are usually well known – ask at your local museum, library, or university.

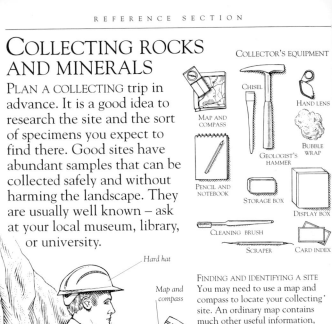

COLLECTOR'S EQUIPMENT

MAP AND COMPASS

CHISEL

GEOLOGIST'S HAMMER

HAND LENS

BUBBLE WRAP

PENCIL AND NOTEBOOK

STORAGE BOX

DISPLAY BOX

CLEANING BRUSH

SCRAPER

CARD INDEX

Hard hat

Map and compass

FINDING AND IDENTIFYING A SITE
You may need to use a map and compass to locate your collecting site. An ordinary map contains much other useful information, such as the location of nearby cliffs and beaches. Detailed geological maps showing the position and age of rock structures are also available from specialist shops.

1 RECORDING A SAMPLE
When you find a good sample, make a detailed sketch of its location. Photographs are also useful. Note down the map reference of the site in case you want to collect there again. Make sure that you record different samples separately.

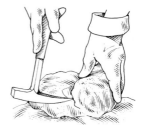

2 REMOVING AND PACKING
If you do take a sample home, chip it out and trim it to size with a hammer. Don't forget your protective gloves and goggles. Wrap each sample using bubble wrap, newspaper, or tissue – this prevents scratching on the journey home.

3 CLEANING AND IDENTIFICATION
At home, unpack and clean your
....
in water – you don't want your samples to dissolve. You may need a hand lens for identification.

4 INDEXING AND STORING
When you have identified your
....
Each specimen needs a label giving its name and original site. An index may be useful for larger collections.

Resources

US

A.E. Seaman Mineralogical Museum
Michigan Technological University
1400 Townsend Drive
Houghton, MI 49931

Academy of Natural Sciences of Philadelphia
1900 Benjamin Franklin Parkway
Philadelphia, PA 19103

American Museum of Natural History
Central Park West at 79th Street
New York, NY 10024

Arizona-Sonora Desert Museum
2021 N. Kinney Road
Tucson, AZ 85743

California Academy of Science
Golden Gate Park
San Francisco, CA 94118

Carnegie Institute of Natural History
4400 Forbes Avenue
Pittsburgh, PA 15213

Cincinnati Museum of Natural History
Union Terminal Building
1301 Western Avenue
Cincinnati, OH 45203

Cleveland Museum of Natural History
1 Wade Oval Drive
University Circle
Cleveland, OH 44106

Cranbrook Institute of Science
1221 N. Woodward Avenue
PO Box 801
Bloomfield Hills, MI 48303

Denver Museum of Natural History
2001 Colorado Boulevard
Denver, CO 80205

Field Museum of Natural History
Roosevelt Road at Lake Shore Drive
Chicago, IL 60605

Geology Museum
Colorado School of Mines
Golden, CO 80401

Harvard Mineralogical and Geological Museum
Harvard University
24 Oxford Street
Cambridge, MA 02138

Houston Museum of Natural Science
1 Hermann Circle Drive
Houston, TX 77030

Lizzadro Museum of Lapidary Art
220 Cottage Hill
Wilder Park
Elmhurst, IL 60126

Maine State Museum
83 State House Station
Augusta, ME 04333

Mineral Museum
University of Arizona
Tucson, AZ 85721

Mineralogical Museum
University of Delaware
101 Penny Hall
Newark, DE 19716

Museum of Geological Sciences
Virginia Polytechnic Institute and State University
2062 Derring Hall
Blacksburg, VA 24061

National Museum of Natural History
Smithsonian Institution
Washington, D.C. 20560

Natural History Museum of Los Angeles County
900 Exposition Boulevard
Los Angeles, CA 90007

New Mexico Bureau of Mines and Mineral Resources Mineral Museum
Campus Station
Socorro, NM 87801

Peabody Museum of Natural History
Yale University
170 Whitney Avenue
New Haven, CT 06511

San Diego Natural History Museum
PO Box 1390
San Diego, CA 92112

Science Museum of Minnesota
30 E. 10th Street
St. Paul, MN 55101

Sterling Hill Mining Museum
30 Plant Street
Ogdensburg, NJ 07439

Journals of interest:

Lapidary Journal
60 Chestnut Avenue
Suite 201
Devon, PA 19533

Mineralogical Record
7413 N. Mowry Place
Tucson, AZ 85741

Rocks & Minerals
Helgreth Publications
1319 18th Street NW
Washington, D.C. 20036

Gems and Minerals
PO Box 687
Mentone, CA 92359

CANADA

Canadian Museum of Nature
National Museum of Canada
240 McLeod Avenue
Ottawa, ONT K1A 0M8

Glenbow Museum
Glenbow Alberta Institute
130 Ninth Avenue S.E.
Calgary, ALB T2G OP3

Nova Scotia Museum of Natural History
1747 Summer Street
Halifax, NS B3H 3A6

Royal Ontario Museum
100 Queen's Park
Toronto, ONT M5S 2C6

M.Y. Williams Geological Museum
University of British Columbia
Vancouver,
BC V6T 1W5

Glossary

ALLOY
A mixture of two types of metal, or a metal and a nonmetal.

ATOM
Smallest part of an element that can exist.

BIOGENIC SEDIMENTARY ROCK
Rock that forms from the fossilized remains of plants and animals.

BOTRYOIDAL HABIT
Rounded, bubbly habit.

CARAT
The standard measure of weight for precious stones and metals. One carat is equivalent to 0.006 oz (0.2 g).

CHATOYANCY
Silky appearance on surface of a mineral. It is also known as the "cat's eye" effect.

CHEMICAL SEDIMENTARY ROCK
Rock that is formed by mineral precipitation.

CLASTS
Fragments in sedimentary rocks that originally formed part of other rocks.

CLEAVAGE
The way a mineral breaks along planes according to its atomic structure.

COMPOUND
Material made up of more than one element.

CONTACT METAMORPHIC ROCK
Rock that forms as the heat from magma or a lava flow alters an existing rock.

CORE
Solid region of iron and nickel that makes up the center of the Earth. It is about 4,320 miles (6,950 km) across.

COUNTRY ROCK
Existing rock that may be sedimentary, igneous or metamorphic.

CRUST
The thin outer layer of the Earth. It is between 4⅓ and 43½ miles (7 and 70 km) thick.

CRYSTAL SYSTEMS
The systems into which crystals are grouped according to symmetry. There are six main crystal systems: cubic, monoclinic, triclinic, trigonal/hexagonal, orthorhombic, and tetragonal.

DENDRITIC HABIT
Branching, or treelike, habit.

DETRITAL SEDIMENTARY ROCK
Rock that is made up of broken fragments of other rocks.

DIAPIR
Large dome of salt beneath the Earth's surface. These structures often trap reserves of oil and gas.

DOUBLE REFRACTION
An optical effect in which an object appears double when viewed through a transparent crystal.

DYKE
Sheet of igneous rock that breaks across existing rock structures.

ELEMENT
Material that cannot be broken down into more simple substances by chemical means.

EROSION
The transportation of material from its original site by processes involving wind, water, and ice.

EVAPORITE
Material left behind when water evaporates.

EXTRUSIVE IGNEOUS ROCK
Igneous rock that forms at the Earth's surface.

FACET
One side of a cut gemstone.

FIBROUS HABIT
Fiberlike habit.

FLUORESCENCE
Optical effect whereby a mineral appears a different color in ultraviolet light than in ordinary daylight.

FOLIATIONS
Patterns caused by aligned crystals in metamorphic rocks.

GEMSTONE
A mineral, usually crystalline, that derives particular value from its color, rarity, and hardness.

GEOLOGIST
A person who studies the Earth.

GRANULAR HABIT
Grainlike habit.

HABIT
The general appearance or shape of a mineral.

HOPPER CRYSTAL
Crystal with regular, stepped depressions on each face.

HYDROTHERMAL VEIN
A crack or fracture in a rock filled with hot, water-rich solutions that flow from underground igneous masses.

IDIOCHROMATIC MINERAL
Mineral that is almost always the same color because of certain light-absorbing atoms that form an essential part of its makeup.

IGNEOUS ROCK
Rock formed as magma cools and hardens in the Earth's crust.

INCLUSION
Crystals of one mineral that are enclosed in crystals of another mineral.

INTRUSIVE IGNEOUS ROCK
Igneous rock that forms beneath the Earth's surface.

IRIDESCENCE
A play of colors on the surface of a mineral like a film of oil on water.

LAVA
Magma at the Earth's surface.

LITHOSPHERE
The Earth's crust and upper mantle. It is approximately 124 miles (200 km) thick.

LUSTER
The way a mineral shines. It is affected by light reflecting off the surface of the mineral.

MAGMA
Molten rock beneath the Earth's surface.

MAGMA CHAMBER
Underground reservoir of magma that feeds a volcano. It can harden to form a pluton.

MANTLE
Layer of the Earth between the core and the crust. It is approximately 1,800 miles (2,900 km) thick.

MASSIVE HABIT
Mineral habit that has no definite shape.

MATRIX
Mass of rock in which crystals are set.

METAMORPHIC ROCK
Rock that forms due to the action of heat and pressure, or heat alone.

METAMORPHISM
The action of heat and pressure.

METEORITE
Object from outer space that survives the passage through the atmosphere to reach Earth.

MINERAL
A solid mixture of chemicals that has certain regular characteristics, such as atomic structure and chemical composition.

MINERAL LODE
Vein of metal ore.

MINERAL VEIN
Cracks in rocks that become filled with hot, mineral-rich liquids.

MOHS' SCALE
Scale devised by the Austrian mineralogist Friedrich Mohs that measures the hardness of minerals by scratching.

NATIVE ELEMENT
Element that occurs naturally in a free state. In other words, it does not form part of a compound.

OOLITH
Small, rounded grains that make up some sedimentary rocks.

OPAQUE MATERIAL
Material that does not allow light to pass through it.

ORE
Rock or other material from which a metal is extracted.

ORGANIC SEDIMENTARY ROCK
Rock that is made up of the remains of plants and trees.

PEGMATITE
Rock, usually igneous, that consists of unusually large crystals.

PERFECT CLEAVAGE
Property of a mineral that breaks only in certain directions.

PIEZOELECTRICITY
Generation of positive and negative charges across a crystal that has pressure applied to it.

PIGMENT
A natural coloring material often used in paints and dyes.

PLATE
Large "panels" that form the Earth's surface.

PLEOCHROISM
Optical property of a mineral where the color of a crystal changes if the crystal is viewed from a different angle.

PLUTON
Large mass of igneous rock that forms beneath the Earth's surface as magma solidifies.

PRECIPITATION
Chemical process whereby a solid substance is deposited from solution in a liquid.

PRISMATIC CRYSTAL
Crystal that is longer in one direction than the other.

RADIOMETRIC DATING
A precise method of dating rocks that measures the rate of decay of radioactive atoms in a rock.

REGIONAL METAMORPHIC ROCK
Rock that forms from the action of heat and pressure on existing rocks, usually in mountain-building areas.

RENIFORM HABIT
Habit that resembles an animal kidney.

ROCK
Solid mixtures, or aggregates, of minerals.

SECONDARY ORE
A mineral or rock that develops from the remains of other ore minerals and thereby becomes an ore itself.

SEDIMENTARY ROCK
Rock that forms at the Earth's surface. It consists of layers of rock fragments or other substances that have been deposited on top of each other.

SILL
Sheet of igneous rock that follows existing rock structures.

SPECIFIC GRAVITY
The comparison of a mineral's weight with the weight of an equal volume of water.

STREAK
The color of a mineral's powder. It is often a more useful identification tool than color because it gives less variable results.

STRIATIONS
Parallel lines on a crystal face that develop as the crystal grows.

STRUCTURAL METAMORPHIC ROCK
Rock that forms in extreme pressure caused by movements in the Earth's crust.

TARNISHING
Chemical reaction that occurs on the surface of a mineral that alters the mineral's characteristic color or luster.

THERMAL METAMORPHIC ROCK
Rock that is altered by the action of heat alone.

TOR
Granite landform characterized by large blocks of rock separated by cracks. The rock originally formed underground, becoming exposed as weathering and erosion removed surrounding rocks.

TRANSLUCENT MATERIAL
Material that allows daylight to pass through it. Objects cannot be seen clearly through a translucent material.

TRANSPARENT MATERIAL
Material that allows daylight to pass through

it. Objects can be seen clearly through a transparent mineral.

TWINNED CRYSTALS
Two or more crystals of the same mineral that intersect each other along a common, or shared, plane.

VESICLE
A rounded cavity in extrusive igneous rocks that is left by a gas bubble as the rock hardens.

VOLCANIC BOMB
Blob of lava thrown out of a volcano. It solidifies before hitting the ground.

VOLCANIC VENT
Central passage in a volcano through which magma flows and erupts as lava.

VULCANIZATION
The process of adding sulfur to rubber products to make them stronger and more durable.

WEATHERING
The breaking down of rocks by the action of rain or processes like freezing, thawing, and dissolving in water.

Index

A

actinolite, 77
aegirine, 101, 136, 140
agate, 48, 49
aggregate, 13
alabaster, 42, 43
albite, 50, 136, 140
alloys, 78-9, 83
almandine garnet, 88, 89, 119, 136, 140
amethyst, 46, 47, 136, 140
ammonites, 17, 68
amphiboles, 77, 98-9, 137
amphibolite, 98
andalusite, 121
anthracite, 133
apatite, 143
aquamarine, 44, 45, 136, 140
asbestos, 99
atomic pattern, 19
augite, 100, 136, 140
axinite, 22
azurite, 23, 70-1, 136, 140

B

barite, 22, 40-1, 136, 140
Barringer crater, Arizona, 115
basalt, 30, 73, 100, 101, 104, 112-13, 114
beryl, 22, 44-5, 74, 136, 140
biogenic sedimentary rocks, 125
biotite, 13, 53, 106, 118, 119, 136, 140
bismuth, 23
bituminous coal, 133

Black Cuillins, Skye, 111
"black jack," 86
blende, 86
Blue John, 90
brass, 79, 87
breccia, 26, 27, 126-7
bronze, 79, 83

C

calcite, 38-9, 136, 140
    breccia, 127
    emerald in, 45
    formation, 21
    hardness, 142
    lapis lazuli, 95
    limestone, 130
    marble, 123
Cambrian period, 144
carat, 35
carbon, 60-1, 120, 121, 132-3
Carboniferous period, 145
Carcassonne, France, 129
carnelian, 48
cassiterite, 82-3, 136, 140
catalytic converters, 59
cat's whisker radios, 63
celestine, 23
chalcedony, 48-9, 136, 140
chalcopyrite, 13, 68-9, 78-9, 136, 140
chalk, 125, 131
chlorine, 37
chlorite, 120
chondrites, 16, 115
chromdravite, 74, 136, 140
chromium, 44, 55

chrysoprase, 48
cinnabar, 23, 84-5, 136, 140
citrine, 47, 136
clay, 120, 132
cleavage, 19, 53, 62, 98, 121
clinoclase, 25
coal, 125, 132-3
cockscomb barite, 40
color, 23, 24-5, 30
comets, 114, 115
compasses, 96
conglomerate, 31, 126
continents, 14-15
cooling, crystal formation, 30
copper, 78-9, 136, 140
    alloys, 83, 87
    chalcopyrite, 13, 69
    malachite, 70
    turquoise, 93
coral, 125, 130
cordierite, 121
core, Earth's, 14, 15
corundum, 24, 54-5, 136, 140, 143
country rocks, 117
Cretaceous period, 144
crocidolite, 99
crust, Earth's, 14, 15, 46, 104, 106, 110, 112
crystal systems, 22
Curie, Pierre and Jacques, 47

D

daisy gypsum, 42
Damour, 76
dating rocks, 17

Dead Sea, 36
Delabole butterflies, 121
dendrites, 56
Derbyshire Spar, 90
desert roses, 41
detrital rocks, 125
Devonian period, 144
diamond, 34-5, 60-1, 136, 140, 143
diapirs, 37
dinosaurs, 17, 144, 145
diopside, 101, 136, 140
dogtooth, 38
dolerite, 98, 104, 112-13
double refraction, 39
dunite, 72
dykes, 105, 116

E
Earth, 14-15
eclogite, 111
elbaite, 74
elements, table of, 138-9
emerald, 22, 44, 45, 136, 140
emery, 55
Empire State Building, New York, 81
enstatite, 101, 136, 140
erosion, 28, 125, 127
evaporites, 124
extrusive rocks, 104, 108, 112

F
feldspar, 50-1
  basalt, 112
  gabbro, 110
  gneiss, 118
  granite, 106, 107
  mica, 19

microcline, 12
orthoclase feldspar, 106, 107, 143
plagioclase feldspar, 110
tourmaline, 74, 75
fieldwork, 146-9
flint, 48, 49, 123, 126
fluorescence, 90
fluorite, 25, 90-1, 136, 140, 142
foliations, 30, 31, 118, 119
fool's gold, 68-9, 79
forging, 97
forsterite, 72, 136, 140
fossils, 17, 31, 68, 121, 125, 129, 131, 144

G
gabbro, 30, 100, 101, 104, 110-11, 112
galena, 20, 38, 56, 57, 62-3, 86, 136, 140
galvanization, 87
garnet, 20, 21, 88-9, 111, 119, 136, 137, 140, 141
gemstones, 13, 21, 82, 106
geological timescale, 144-5
Giant's Causeway, Northern Ireland, 113
glaciers, 127
glaucophane, 99, 137, 141
gneiss, 27, 31, 117, 118-19
gold, 24, 64-5, 68, 137, 141
granite, 12, 13, 26, 30, 50, 75, 104, 105, 106-7, 118
graphic granite, 107
graphite, 60-1, 137, 141
Great Bear Lake, Canada, 119
grossular garnet, 88, 137, 141

gunpowder, 67
gypsum, 22, 24, 42-3, 137, 141, 142

H
halite, 25, 36-7, 137, 141
Hauy, Abbé, 53
heliodor, 44, 137, 141
hematite, 20, 25, 51, 80-1, 137, 141
hopper crystals, 37
hornblende, 98-9, 118, 137, 141
hydrothermal veins 62, 82, 90

I
idocrase, 22
igneous rocks, 21, 26, 28, 30, 98, 100, 104-15
intrusive rocks, 104
iridescence, 25, 51, 81
iron, 44, 45, 53, 54, 80-1, 96-7, 114

J
jade, 76-7
jadeite, 76-7, 137, 141
jasper, 48
jewelry, 34, 47, 56, 57, 58, 65, 76, 88, 94, 92
Jurassic period, 145

K
kerogen, 132
kidney ore, 80-1
Kel ... ...
kimberlite, 34
Kiruna, Sweden, 96
Kohoutek, comet, 115

L
labradorite, 25, 51, 137, 141
lapidary, 34-5
lapis lazuli, 94-5
lava, 21, 26, 29, 73, 105, 108, 109, 112, 113
lazurite, 94-5, 137, 141
lead, 20, 38, 62, 63, 83
lepidolite, 18
lignite, 133
limestone, 21, 27, 31, 38-9, 94, 122, 123, 125, 127, 130-1
lithosphere, 14
lodes, 100
lodestone, 96
luster, 23

M
magma, 14, 15, 21, 26, 28-9, 72, 104-5, 106, 107, 108, 110, 116
magnesium, 53, 72
magnetite, 21, 96-7, 110, 137, 141
malachite, 24, 25, 70-1, 137, 141
manganese, 44
mantle, Earth's, 14, 15, 101, 104
marble, 88, 94, 99, 116, 122-3
marcasite, 68, 137, 141
mercury, 84-5, 137, 141
metamorphic rocks, 21, 26-7, 29, 30-1, 60, 76, 82, 88, 116-23
meteorites, 96, 101, 114-15
micas, 13, 18, 19, 52-3, 75, 106, 119, 120
microcline, 12, 106

microgranite, 104
migmatite, 118
Mijas marble, 122
millet-seed sandstone, 31, 129
minerals:
  age, 16-17
  composition, 138-41
  formation, 20-1
  hardness, 142-3
  identifying, 22-3
  table of, 136-7
  types, 12-13, 18-19
Mohs' scale of hardness, 23, 142-3
Moon rocks, 100, 114
moonstone, 51
morganite, 44, 137, 141
mountain leather, 99
mountains, 15, 21, 27, 117, 127
muscovite, 52, 119, 137, 141
mylonite, 117

N
nail-head calcite, 38
nephrite, 76-7, 137, 141
New Hebrides Islands, 73
nickel, 15, 58, 114
nuclear fission, 60

O
obsidian, 104, 105, 108-9
ocean ridges, 14
ochre, 80
oil, 132
olivine, 20-1, 72-3, 110-11, 112, 114-15, 123, 137, 141
oolitic limestone, 27, 130
opal, 48, 137, 141

Ordovician period, 144
ores, 13, 106
organic sedimentary rocks, 125
orthoclase feldspar, 106, 107, 143
oysters, 38, 87

P
Pamukkale Falls, Turkey, 39
Peacock Throne, 55
pearls, 38
peat, 26, 133
pegmatites, 19, 44, 75, 106
"Pele's hair," 73
peridot, 72-3
Permian period, 145
pewter, 83
piezoelectricity, 46, 47
Pisa, Leaning Tower of, Italy, 123
plagioclase feldspar, 110
plaster of Paris, 42, 43
plates, Earth's crust, 14-15, 29
platinum, 23, 58-9, 100, 137, 141
pleochroism, 75
plutons, 104, 105, 116
porphyritic basalt, 112
potassium, 37
Pre-Cambrian period, 144
puddingstone, 126
pyrite, 22, 31, 68-9, 95, 120, 121, 137, 141
pyrope garnet, 88, 89, 137, 141
pyroxenes, 15, 76, 100-1, 110, 111, 112, 115, 136, 137
pyroxenite, 100

Q

quarries, 13, 121
Quaternary period, 145
quartz, 12-13, 137
  chemical formula, 141
  colours, 24
  crystalline, 46-7
  gneiss, 118
  gold, 65
  granite, 106-7
  hardness, 143
  mica pegmatites, 19
  non-crystalline, 48-9
  sandstone, 128-9
  tourmaline and, 74-5

R

radiometric dating, 17
Ramses II, 107
realgar, 20
regional metamorphism, 117
rhombic cleavage, 98
rhyolite, 108-9
riebeckite, 99, 137, 141
rock salts, 36-7
rocks:
  age, 16-17
  identifying, 30-1
  minerals and, 12-13
  rock cycle, 28-9
  types, 26-7
rubellite, 74
ruby, 24, 25, 54-5, 137, 141
Ruskin, John, 75

S

safety, 146-7
Sahara Desert, 128

sand, 46
sandstone, 31, 124, 128-9
sapphire, 24, 54, 137, 141
schist, 31, 89, 118-19
schorl, 75, 137, 141
sedimentary rocks, 16-17, 21, 26-7, 29, 30-1, 124-33
selenite, 22, 42, 43
serpentinite, 99, 111
shale, 120, 132
shells, 38, 124, 125, 131
silica, 30, 52, 104, 105, 106, 108
sills, 105, 116
Silurian period, 144
silver, 24, 56-7, 62, 63, 137, 141
slate, 31, 120-1
Slyudyanka, Russian Federation, 13
Smith, William, 17
snowflake obsidian, 108
sodium, 37
specific gravity, 23
specular hematite, 81
sphalerite, 86-7, 137, 141
spinel, 21
stalactites, 39
stalagmites, 39
steel, 81, 91
stone forest, Kunming, China, 131
stony iron, 114
strata, 124
streak, 23
sulfur, 24, 60-1, 94, 137, 141
sunstone, 51
sylvite, 21, 36-37, 137, 141

T

talc, 23, 142
tektites, 115
Tertiary period, 145
thermometers, 85
tiger's eye, 24
tin, 78, 82-3
titanium, 54
topaz, 143
tors, 107
tourmaline, 13, 25, 74-5, 106, 136, 137, 141
transparency, 23
tremolite, 77, 99, 137, 141
Triassic period, 145
turquoise, 25, 92-3, 137, 141

U

ultramarine, 94, 95
ultraviolet light, 90

V

vanadium, 44
veins, 20, 46, 84, 106
vermiculite, 18
vermilion, 84
vesicles, 113
volcanic bombs, 73, 96
volcanoes, 29, 66-7, 73, 104-5, 112-13

W

watches, 55, 87
weathering, 28
wood tin, 83

Z

Zebirget, 72
zinc, 78, 86-7

Acknowledgments

Dorling Kindersley would like to thank:

Hilary Bird for the index, Esther Labi for editorial assistance, John Betts, Camela Decaire, Ray Rogers, John Sampson White.

Photographs by:

Michael Crockett, Geoff Dann, Andreas von Einsiedel, Steve Gorton, Chas Howson, Colin Keates, Dave King, James Stevenson, Harry Taylor.

Illustrations by:

John Woodcock, Dan Wright.

Picture credits: t = top b = bottom c = center l= left r = right
Archiv fur Kunst/ Museo di Argenti, Florence 94 bl. Bergakademie Freiberg 142tr. Christie's Images 45cb. Stephanie Colasanti 131tr. Archive P. et M. Curie 46bc. The Environmental Picture Library/ Graham Burns 13br. ffotograff /Patricia Aithie 131br. Robert Harding Picture Library 67 tr; 77tl; 111bl; 119 br/ Ian Griffiths 107tl;/Tomlinson 41c; Adam Woolfitt 92bl; 128tl. Michael Holford 55bl; 89tl; 93tr. Geoscience Features 82br. Image Bank/ Jeff Bartel 121 tr;/Jackie Gucia 128bl;/Johnson 134-135. Impact /Mike McQueen 107br;/Tony Page 123bc;/ David Palmer 108 tr/Homer Sykes 91tl; 132bl. Johnson Mathey 59tl. Mansell Collection 17cr; 53tr; 75 cl. Biblioteca Medicea Laurenziana, Florence 65tr. NASA 114bl; 115c; 115br, National Nuclear Corporation 60bl. Royal Museum of Scotland/ Michel Zabé 57br. Science Photo Library/Jim Amos 100bl;/Alex Bartel 121tr;/Jack Fields 73 tl;/David Leah 57tr;/Peter Manzel 50 bc;/N.A.S.A. 16bl;/Soames Summerhays 113tr. Still Pictures/ Roger Stenberg 96 br. Tony Stone/John Freeman 113bl/ Jacky Gucin 128bl. Wallace Collection 49b.

Every effort has been made to trace the copyright holders and we apologize in advance for any unintentional omissions. We would be pleased to insert the appropriate acknowledgement in any subsequent edition of this publication.